The
Power of
Oneness

The information in this book is designed to help you make informed decisions. If you suspect that you have a problem that might require professional treatment or advice, seek qualified assistance. The personal stories in this book are true; however, the names are fictitious.

Published by The Power of Oneness, LLC
P.O. Box 176
Gwynedd Valley, PA 19437
www.thepowerofoneness.com

Distributed by Greenleaf Book Group LLC
For ordering information or special discounts for bulk purchases, please contact Greenleaf Book Group at PO Box 91869, Austin, TX 78709, 512.891.6100.

Cover design by Benjamin Hill

Cataloging-in-Publication data
(Prepared by The Donohue Group, Inc.)
Brossman, Sandra C.
    [Awakening to oneness. 2012]
    The power of oneness : live the life you choose / Sandra Brossman. -- 3rd ed.
    p. ; cm.
    Issued also as an ebook.
    First edition published as: Awakening to oneness. Aurora, OH : Greenleaf Book Group, c2001.
    ISBN: 978-0-9858795-0-1
    1. Self-realization. 2. Spiritual life. 3. Success. I. Title. II. Title: Awakening to oneness
BF637.S4 B6377 2012
158.1   2012912898

Part of the Tree Neutral® program, which offsets the number of trees consumed in the production and printing of this book by taking proactive steps, such as planting trees in direct proportion to the number of trees used: www.treeneutral.com

Issued also as an audio book, available on Amazon.com, Audible.com, and iTunes
eBook available on Amazon.com and BN.com

Printed in the United States of America on acid-free paper

12 13 14 15 16 17   10 9 8 7 6 5 4 3 2 1

Third Edition, The Power of Oneness
Second Edition, The Power of Oneness, 2003
First Edition, published as Awakening to Oneness, 2001

The Power of Oneness

Live the Life You Choose™

Sandra Brossman

P.O. Box 176, Gwynedd Valley, PA 19437

To My Daughter, Erin McCue,
my beautiful child, and greatest gift,
who inspires me to love unconditionally

To My Husband, Len Bezar,
my loving, supportive partner and friend,
who enthusiastically shares my Vision of Oneness

To My Parents, John and Kathryn Brossman,
whose lives exemplified the qualities of
kindness, simplicity, and integrity

To All Whose Lives Are Touched by this Book,
may they be blessed by its contents

An Acknowledgment of Thanks to:

Len Bezar, my husband and best friend, who has always believed in me, supported me through all the ups and downs, and filled in all the spaces when I have needed help.

Erin McCue, my amazing daughter, who bravely stepped into the monumental challenge of getting the message of this book to the world at large by contributing the brilliance of her business and Internet technology expertise.

Johanna Walters, my angelic business partner and very special friend, for her extraordinary contribution of business wisdom, financial generosity, and countless hours of preparation to manifest our mutual dream of sharing the message of The Power of Oneness with the world.

Suzanne Chirieleison, my lovely sister, for her valuable feedback as I wrote this book, and, more importantly, for her unconditional love and friendship throughout my whole life.

Andrew Molnar and Marie Skweir, my dear soul-mate friends, for courageously traveling this spiritual journey on earth with me and demonstrating their commitment to the message of love in this book by the way they live their lives.

Bruce Masi, my loyal friend, whose logic, wit, and scientific insights both ground and inspire me.

The Circle of Light, a spiritual community of enlightened souls, who are a model of how people can unite their energies to inspire, support, encourage, and amplify each other to bring love, light, and harmony to all that is.

Table of Contents

Introduction xiii

Prologue 1

Chapter Zero—Our Present World

What Is Happening? What Has Changed? 13

Where Do We Begin in Our Healing? 14

Part One—Remembering Our Spiritual Truth

Chapter One—The Nature of Our Whole Self

What Is Our "Whole Self?" 19

What Is a Material World? 20

What Is a Non-Material World? 22

What Is Energy? 23

If We Cannot Perceive Energy With Our

Five Senses, How Do We Know That It Exists? 25

What Is the Importance of Recognizing

We Are Energy? 28

Chapter Two—We Create Our Reality

What Is Personal Reality? 30

What Is Our Collective Reality? 30

Why Are Our Thoughts So Powerful? 31

Is It Really Possible to Change Our

Personal Reality by Changing Our Thoughts? 35

What Are Perceptions? 36

If We Can Change Our Reality with

the Conscious Choice of Our Thoughts,

Why Don't We Just Change Our Thinking? 37

Even if We Are Willing to Take Responsibility for Our Choice

of Perceptions, Aren't There Certain Conditions In Life over

Which We Have No Human Control? 37

What Is Perspective? 39
How Is Our Collective World Perspective
    Expanding? 41

Chapter Three—The Perspective of Separation
How Does the Perspective of Separation Help Us
    Embrace the Meaning of Life? 44
What Does Living from the "Outside-in" Mean? 45
Why Does Living from the Outside-in Contract
    Our Energy? 48
Why Have So Many of Us Chosen this Perspective
    of Life? 50
How Do We Move Beyond the Perspective
    of Separation? 51
How Does the Perspective of Separation Affect Our
    Inner Spirit? 51
How Does the Perspective of Separation Affect
    Our Bodies? 52
How Does the Perspective of Separation Affect
    Our Minds? 53
What Is Meant by Our "World Brain?" 59
How Can We Possibly Interpret the Turmoil We Are
    Experiencing As a Sign That Our Society Is
    Moving Toward the Perspective of Oneness? 60

Chapter Four—The Perspective of Oneness
How Do We Know What Our Inner Spiritual
    Truth Is? 70
What Does Living From the "Inside-Out" Mean? 72
What Is Oneness of Spirit? 75
Is Spirituality the Same Thing As Religion? 77
What Is Unconditional Love? 78
What Is a Sacred Life? 79

What Is Conditional Love? 81

Why Do We Have to Love Ourselves in Order to
   Love Someone Else Unconditionally? 83

How Can We Effectively Help Others? 85

What Is the Light Within? 88

Part Two—Healing Our Past

Chapter Five—Opening to Change—Forgiveness

Isn't It Important That We Remember the Past? 94

Why Do We Fear Change? 94

How Does Pain Serve As a Messenger of Truth? 97

Why Is It Essential That We Release the Past? 100

What Is Forgiveness? 100

Is It Necessary to Be in the Physical Presence of
   Those Whom We Need to Forgive? 102

If Forgiveness Is So Essential to Our Healing Process,
   Why Is It So Hard to Do? 104

There Are So Many Forgiveness Issues—Where Do
   We Begin? 106

Even If We Can Forgive Ourselves How Is It
   Humanly Possible to Forgive People
   Who Have Hurt Us Deeply? 106

How Can We Send Out Thoughts of Forgiveness? 108

Chapter Six—Becoming Aware of Our Basic Beliefs

Where Do Our Basic Beliefs Originate? 112

Why Do We Need to Know Our Basic Beliefs? 112

How Can We Become Conscious of Which Basic
   Beliefs Are Blocking Our Potential? 114

Self-Evaluation—Basic Beliefs Underlying Our
   Perceptions of Life 116

Why Do We Hold onto Self-Defeating
   Basic Beliefs? 120

Self-Sabotaging Behaviors—Seven Ways To Stay
Stuck In Our Emotional Pain 122
Chapter Seven—Choosing Basic Beliefs of Oneness
Why Are Affirmations So Effective at
Reprogramming Our Basic Beliefs? 129
How Do We Construct Powerful and Effective
Affirmations? 131
How Do We Transform Our Feelings of Separation
into Affirmations of Oneness? 134
Transforming Perceptions of Separation Into
Affirmations of Oneness 136

Part Three—Awakening to Oneness
Chapter Eight—Creating Visions of Our Desired Reality
What Is the Purpose of Creating Visions? 144
How Do We Know What We Want to Envision? 144
How Can Visions Make Our Dreams Come True? 145
How Do We Create Powerful, Energizing
Vision Statements? 147
What Are Some Examples of
Dynamic Vision Statements 152
Are Vision Statements the Same Thing As
Affirmations? 154
What Are Some Ways in Which We Can
Reinforce Our Visions? 154
What Are Some Suggestions for Incorporating Vision
Statements into Meditation/Visualizations? 156
What About Those of Us Who Do Not See
Mental Pictures? 157
How Do Visions Expand Our Energy? 157
What Is Meant by "Remaining Open?" 159
Are Visions Synonymous with Goals? 161
Aren't Visions Unrealistic? 163

Is It Really Possible to Create a Whole New
    Reality through Visions? 164
How Can We Strengthen Our Commitment to
    Envisioning New Realities? 166
What If Our Visions Don't Seem to Be
    Manifesting? 170
Is It Possible to Create Visions In a Conscious
    State of Mind? 173

Chapter Nine—Integration

What Are the Qualities of Oneness? 176
What Is the Experience of a World of Oneness? 176
If It Is Divine Will That We Experience the
    Qualities of Oneness, Why Are We Not
    Experiencing Them In Our Present Physical
    Existence? 180
Do We Really Have the Human Capability
    to Co-Create a Physical World Which Is Ideal? 181
How Do We Find the Time and Space to Pray
    in This Busy Day and Age? 181
Is There a Certain Way to Pray? 182
How Do We Co-Create? 183
Creating Vision Prayers 186
Isn't It Best to Reserve Our Prayers for the Really
    Important Things? 192
What about Praying for Others? 193
How Can Simply Praying Change the
    Physical Nature of a Situation? 196
What Is Mindfulness? 199
What Is Synchronicity? 200
We Are All a Part of a Global Transformation 203
A Vision of Oneness 205

Introduction

The book you are about to read is a spiritual book. Because the word "spiritual" may have different connotations for each of us, I feel it is important to clarify what the word *spirit* really means. The Latin root word of spirit is *spiritus*, which literally means *breath*.

Remembering this helps us to release the perception that spirituality is a remote concept separate from our physical reality or that it is synonymous with religion. It also helps us to realize that there is no such thing as a "non-spiritual person"—the simple truth is that if we breathe we qualify as being spiritual.

With this in mind, this book applies to everyone—everyone, that is, who is committed to taking responsibility for *truly healing* his or her life. True healing requires that we are open to reaching beneath the outer symptoms of the pain and disease that we are experiencing individually and as a society by choosing to work from the inside out—from the core level of our being. Because spiritual healing acknowledges the whole person, it automatically has a positive effect on our mental, emotional, and physical well being.

During the course of my career as a holistic healer and business consultant, I have often been approached by people who say that even though they are awakening to their spiritual nature, they do not know how to go about actually implementing spiritual values into their everyday lives. *The Power of Oneness* addresses this need by offering practical tools that empower you to remember your spiritual truth, heal your past, and consciously manifest the quality of life you choose to live in this physical world.

There are many ways to use this book. You may decide to follow the flow in which the book is presented. If you are experiencing a great deal of emotional pain, you may choose to begin with Part Two, which deals with personal healing, and then return to Part One; or you may prefer to trust your intuition and open the book to any page. If you feel challenged when reading certain parts of this book, it is helpful to remember that feeling stuck and uncomfortable is usually an indication that we are facing exactly what we most need to embrace in order to expand our spiritual growth. The important thing is to persist while being patient and gentle with yourself.

Because this book is about Oneness, it is presented in parts in order to understand the whole of our true nature:

Part One—Remembering Our Spiritual Truth (Chapters One through Four): These chapters, slightly technical in nature, discuss the universal principles that lay the foundation for understanding our creative human nature and how the energy of our thoughts, words, and actions create our physical reality. We are reminded of how our choices of perception determine whether we live from the *outside-in*, a perspective of using our energy to survive our outer world, or the *inside-out*, a perspective of consciously using our energy to create a better world by centering our lives around our inner spiritual values.

Part Two—Healing Our Past (Chapters Five through Seven): These chapters are more personal in that we apply the spiritual truth principles discussed in Part One to our individual lives. We are guided through a healing process, starting with opening our minds to change. We heal our emotional wounds from the past through forgiveness and identify the self-limiting basic beliefs to which we cling, as well as the self-sabotaging behaviors that reinforce our fears. This clears us to choose healthy beliefs which enable us to create the quality of life we want to experience.

Part Three—Awakening To Oneness (Chapters Eight and Nine): These chapters discuss our inner power to integrate spiritual values into our physical existence through the power of visions. We are guided through a dynamic visions process which demonstrates how we can consciously use our energy to manifest our ideal reality. Together, we remember our magnificent potential to work in concert with each other and divine will to co-create an inner and outer world of love and truth.

I invite you to take a deep breath and to open your heart and mind to what you are about to read. The pages within this book are about universal truths which you already know but perhaps, like many of us, have forgotten. In order to remember, I encourage you to use your eyes not only to see what is in front of you and what you can touch, but also to look above and below, within and without, and beyond where we presently are, for it is in this space of openness that we allow ourselves to truly awaken.

Prologue

It was an afternoon in March of 1996. I was in the process of bringing closure to a lengthy consulting project and basking in thoughts of enjoying some leisure time when the telephone rang. It was one of my keenly insightful friends calling me.

"I keep having this strong feeling you are going to write a book," she said.

"What is the book about?" I asked.

"I haven't the slightest idea," she replied, "I'm sure you'll figure it out."

We both laughed. This type of exchange is so typical of our relationship. For years we have relished in the joy of sharing the many wonderful, loving, spiritual messages we receive when we pray and meditate. We have come to realize that these intuitive messages are always of truth, and yet they have the somewhat disconcerting habit of coming through as mysterous clues asking to be explored.

Seeing the amazing blessings that have come into my life over the years by listening to my intuition has confirmed my trust in the validity of spiritual messages countless times. Like many people, my spiritual awakening came in the midst of a major personal trauma. My wake-up call occurred many years ago when a divorce threw me into a tailspin and my life came down in a crash landing. Within a period of three months I lost my husband, my home, my business of ten years, and all of my material possessions. In the midst of all of this, I was raising my three-year-old daughter by myself and receiving no financial support. Coping with an understandably confused and angry child, working a lot of extra hours learning a new job, dealing with a mountain of bills, and struggling with my own emotional issues brought on an acute and chronic bout with asthma. To say that I was feeling angry and discouraged about life would be an optimistic statement. I remember feeling so overwhelmed at one point that I broke into tears at the pressure of having to decide which clothes to put into each pile as I sorted out the laundry. Feeling that my world had ended, I completely surrendered my life to a higher spiritual power. In that moment I learned that, indeed, my world, as I had known it, had ended, but only to create the space for a new and far more meaningful one.

My life has taken on a whole new direction since that day, and the blessings from my shift in consciousness emanating from that crisis continue to grace every area of my life. The greatest blessing was that I began to learn the remarkable power of prayer. I have to say that I did not pray out of any religious convictions. Quite honestly, my motivation to pray was out of sheer desperation and the feeling that I was out of options. Even so, it quickly became apparent to me that the more I prayed, the more I experienced a synchronous flow of everything I needed appearing at the perfect time.

One aspect of my life that reflected this flow of abundance was my career. Within eighteen months I obtained a large consulting contract, enabling me not only to get out of debt, but also to start up another business consulting practice and experience great financial comfort. As my own spiritual growth has evolved, so also has the nature of my career. I have been greatly inspired to become certified in many body-mind-spirit natural healing processes, and now have a private practice in holistic healing and spiritual counseling. Witnessing the miraculous spiritual healings within the lives of the many people with whom I have worked over the years has also motivated me to organize a company specializing in the facilitation of personal and corporate spiritual workshops. These workshops focus on an amazing *visions process* which enables us to consciously create what we want to experience in our lives by accessing and acting upon our personal inner wisdom, a process which I share in the latter part of this book. Another blessing which came into my life seven years after my crisis was that I met and married a wonderful man who brought his lovely children and grandchildren into our family.

With all this in mind, I was confused by the inner resistance I felt as I hung up from the phone conversation with my friend. I've learned to be very open to spiritual messages—but write a book? Immediately the self-doubts began to surface—the kind most of us have when we are being invited to expand ourselves by stretching into new areas with which we are totally unfamiliar. The internal dialogue began to gear up.

"I don't have time." "I don't know how to write a book." "What am I supposed to write about?" "Why me?" These were just a few of the questions and excuses I offered myself.

I quieted my thoughts by reassuring myself that if this were truth, the message would be reinforced in other ways. I feel confident about this because I have learned that The Divine has infinite patience in providing us with as many opportunities as we require to help us remember why we came to this earth.

Two weeks went by when one morning another friend, whom I had not spoken with for several months, called.

"Hi, are you working on a book?" she asked intently.

"No, I'm not. Why do you ask that?" I responded.

"It's weird," she continued. "I had this very clear dream last night. I saw you carrying a notebook around with you. You were taking prolific notes. I'm almost positive you were writing a spiritual book of some kind."

After I hung up from our conversation, I sat down and said a simple prayer: "Okay, I am willing and open to honor my spiritual purpose in whatever ways I am asked. If it is divine will that I write a book, please verify this for me in ways that I can understand."

Within a few days of saying this prayer I found myself feeling much more open to at least considering the idea of writing a book. I also began to have constant dreams about visiting Sedona, Arizona. While I was aware that Sedona is a highly sacred location, I knew very little about it at that time, so I didn't understand why I was feeling this strong, sudden need to go to Sedona specifically.

It didn't take long to find out why. Within a week of my prayer, my husband, who is also a consultant, bounded into the house from the mailbox and announced to me that we had just received an invitation to make a joint presentation at a business conference.

"Guess where the conference is going to be?" he asked excitedly.

"Arizona!" we blurted out in unison.

The day of the conference arrived and we delivered our presentation. At the end of the session, we were encircled by a few people who had remained to ask questions. A young man whom I'd never seen before excused himself as he stepped through the group to hand me a business card.

"After you write your book, call this person—she will help you," he said simply and then quietly disappeared.

I hadn't mentioned the book. How could he know?

"Did you tell anyone about the book?" I asked my husband, Len.

"No, and I've never seen that man before," he answered quickly.

I felt a warm electrical sensation moving up my spine and the definite feeling that I had just received an answer to my prayer requesting confirmation.

Participating in the conference in Tucson paid for our transportation expenses and enabled us to easily take a side trip to Sedona for five days. During that time, we visited the vortexes, enjoyed the awesome beauty, and assimilated the powerful energy of this great spiritual site. I knew I was being prepared to write this book, but I didn't know specifically how. I also realized it didn't matter whether I understood or not—I knew I was exactly where I needed to be. I returned home from Sedona feeling rested and inspired.

From that point on, things became much more clear. Whether I was praying, sitting in meditation, taking a walk, or doing the dishes, the intuitive messages started pouring through. I began to sense a loving spiritual energy guiding me to write a book with a broad, positive view of the spiritual relevance underlying the confusion which most of us are experiencing within our personal lives and society at large. I was told that this book is to remind myself and others of our magnificent human ability to create new realities simply by changing our perceptions, and that we all have the innate human potential to access universal truth by listening to the voice of our inner spirit. Most importantly: *The time is* now *to act upon our spiritual truth.*

There were many times during the course of writing this book when I felt I would have been more comfortable delivering the above message through a warm, personalized style of writing; however, my inner guidance persistently prevailed upon me to stress, in a firm and loving way, that it is critical to the welfare of the world that we each take responsibility for acting upon our inner truth, starting in this moment. Accordingly, this book is written for those of us who are at a point in life when we are truly willing to take personal responsibility for healing our lives. It is a book that moves beyond merely providing us with spiritual insights—it also guides us through a personal healing process that requires us to take action upon our awareness.

During prayer and meditations, I continued to feel a flow of very specific guidance. This book is to be practical and particularly sensitive to those who perhaps would not typically read a book on spirituality, such as: those who feel that spiritual books do not mesh with their left-brain, logical perspective of life; people who feel that spirituality is too esoteric to think about as they endure their day-to-day struggles to survive; or perhaps those who feel a knot in their stomachs at the mere mention of the word "spirituality" because it triggers childhood memories of religious dogma with which they are still struggling.

More specific guidance continued. The book is to be written predominantly in the collective first person, "we," so as to minimize any separation between the writer and reader. This made sense to me. It is also to have ten chapters, and start with zero. This did not make sense to me.

"Why zero?" I asked my then seventeen-year-old daughter, never realizing she had the answer right on the tip of her tongue.

"Of course, it makes perfect sense!" she said in her bright, youthful manner as she began to fire off the logic of it.

"We learned that in mathematical theory! Between any two numbers, such as zero and one, there are an infinite number of points which exist but are not necessarily seen. You are probably going to talk about an infinite number of points in this book which people do not actually see with their eyes. Anyway, how could you possibly discuss the process of life without looking at an entire cycle, which begins and ends with zero? I've got to run now—I'm in a hurry," she ends . . .

Phew! Asked and answered. Who says teenagers don't know what's going on in the world? My daughter's insight reminded me that in order to make changes we have to begin where we are, at zero point. Accordingly, this book begins with Chapter Zero.

The guidance continued, but I began to receive it in a fully conscious state of mind. I was told that it is essential that I not only acknowledge, but *honor* the differences in all people. The main word here is *all*, irrespective of our religious and philosophical perceptions. This book is to emphasize not our differences, but what we all have in common—we all have a spiritual connection with a higher reality. What we each call this higher reality is a matter of our personal beliefs, depending on where we are on our spiritual path; therefore, throughout the book I have referred to our ultimate creative source in general terms, such as "Supreme Being," so that each of us is free to embrace the unconditional love of the universe in his and her own way.

As I sat down at the computer with a blank page staring at me, I wondered where to begin. As soon as I committed myself to show up at the computer each day and simply listen, the input for the book started coming in from everywhere. It definitely was not automatic writing—where one records a stream of consciousness which comes through while in an altered state. Instead, I found I was required to be in a fully conscious state, completely mindful of the fact that I would receive all the information I needed for this book the way all of life is revealed—one moment at a time. My job was to be open to receiving, organizing, synthesizing, and documenting the flow of wisdom coming through me and to me.

Where did the input for this book come from? First and foremost, I received specific information through lucid dreams almost every night during the entire two-year period of writing this book. Usually the dreams contained the answers to the very questions which were on my mind as I fell asleep. Also, a large portion of the content is a synthesis of information I have intuitively received throughout many years of prayer and meditation. Since the book is about integration, I called upon both my left-brain pragmatic experiences as a business cosultant in the corporate world, as well as my right-brain extraordinary experiences as a spiritual healer and facilitator of vision workshops. Additionally, I received input from work-shops that I attended, such as the wonderful Empowerment Workshops conducted by Gail Straub and David Gershon; interviews with people in all walks of life; every-day conversations with my family, clients, friends, and strangers; and books that found their way into my hands. It seemed that everywhere I turned, people were waiting to provide me with exactly what I most needed to know at exactly the right time. Not surprisingly, I found myself carrying a note-book everywhere I went, just as my friend had envisioned.

It also became apparent that I was not going to be able to just write about things in this book. I discovered in short order that I was actually required to *experience* whatever I was writing about. Sometimes this was in painful ways, as when I wrote the chapter on forgiveness. Within a day of my writing the forgiveness exercise, someone hurt me deeply and I was called upon to practice what I had just written, allowing me to see, first-hand, that the exercise is profoundly effective. On the other hand, I also experienced what I was writing about in wonderful ways, such as the bliss I experienced when I was writing the last chapter on integration.

The process of writing this book has confirmed for me that life is a spiritual treasure hunt—when we are paying attention, we see that there are clues everywhere we look, guiding us to stay on our path toward wholeness. This is not to say that I have not had many periods of feeling frustrated and overwhelmed; but even in those moments of uncertainty,

I have been provided with reassuring "clues"—such as the time that summer when I found myself staring at the wall, feeling greatly discouraged. I knew I had been asked to simplify the information I was receiving as much as possible, but I was experiencing, first hand, that simplification can be a very complicated process. I began to wrestle with self-doubt, so I prayed for confirmation. I recall that my specific request was quick and to the point: "Please help me to know, am I writing this book in the correct way? Please send me a sign to indicate if I am on the right track."

It was a warm and sunny summer day, so I shut down my computer and headed for the local swimming pool. As I was standing in the water, I could not help but notice a frail, elderly gentleman cautiously entering the pool. He slowly swam in my direction.

As he approached me he asked, "Are you sending energy to me? I have Parkinson's Disease, and I usually can't swim, yet I feel tremendous energy today. For some reason, I feel very drawn to you."

I smiled as I suggested to him that he was probably feeling the energy of the beautiful day. I reminded him that the energy of life is everywhere and is always available to us.

"That's an interesting insight," he said. "What do you do for a living?"

I told him I was a business consultant and holistic health practitioner and that I was presently working on a book.

"What are you writing about?" he inquired.

"Spirituality," I answered briefly.

"Is that the same thing as religion?"

"No," I responded, "it is not the same thing. Religion is an organization of people who share in the same beliefs about life. Each one of us can choose which religion we belong to, or whether we want to belong to any religion at all. Spirit is not something we have to decide about—we have all been chosen by being blessed with a spirit—spirit is the breath of life and the essence of love."

He closed his eyes for at least ten long seconds. "You know what?" he said as he slowly opened his eyes. "It's taken me seventy-five years, but I think I finally understand: Love is not something we get from outside of ourselves. It is the energy of life within and all around us, and I don't have to do anything to qualify for it."

"Wow! You have just grasped the entire meaning of my book!" I exclaimed.

He gazed at me squarely in the eyes, raised his finger in a fatherly fashion, and emphatically directed me, "Now as you write your book, young lady, you remember to present things just as simply as you have for me today. I am here to tell you that you are on the right track!"

Chapter Zero

Our Present World

This book is based on the fundamental spiritual principle that, at a soul level, each one of us has all the answers to our own questions. If this is true, then why are so many of us feeling limited, stuck, confused, and in pain? Why does it appear that our social structures are falling apart? Why are we feeling and seeing so much suffering and hostility within and all around us?

Having entered the twenty-first century and a new millennium, we are sensing a highly-charged current of change which is indiscriminately affecting everyone everywhere. No matter who we are, where we live, or what our role is in life, we are personally feeling the repercussions of a major shift. Many of the social institutions to which we have long subscribed are in a state of great upheaval. Whether it be within the areas of our government, corporate structure, health care system, educational system, religious organizations, or the family unit, the traditional institutions which, for centuries, have been perceived as the mainstays of our lives are no longer providing us with the kind of security for which we long.

These changes are not only in our external existence but within our personal lives as well. Many of us are experiencing turmoil in exactly the areas which, in the past, seemed to have provided us the most stability: job security, personal relationships, positions of power, and financial wealth. There seems to be a relentless hunger deep within us that cannot be satiated by the usual physical gratifications of food, money, power, sex, and fame. It feels as though the very foundation of our security is vanishing!

At the same time, we are at a crossroads in our human development in that the enormous power of our collective intelligence enables us to inflict disastrous damage to our world or to do tremendous good. On one hand, we have the knowledge to annihilate the entire human species through nuclear, chemical, and biological warfare; on the other hand, our technological knowledge gives us the capability to connect with each other on a global level, instantaneously, through the Internet. Is it any wonder we are seeing and feeling a great deal of stress within and all around us?

Fortunately, within the midst of all this chaos something wonderful is happening. We are awakening to a spiritual consciousness which is reminding us of the necessity to use our creativity and knowledge for the greater good of humanity. No matter what our personal beliefs and religious preferences may be, people are becoming increasingly conscious of a loving spiritual force guiding the movement of the universe. Even though we are in the eye of a storm of mass confusion, we are seeing increasing indications of renewed inspiration everywhere we turn! Whether it be at home, in restaurants, in the workplace, in church, or at the mall, there is a rekindled spark in the eyes of more and more people as we are now openly and freely discussing spirituality and the meaning of life. Never before have so many media broadcasts, movies, workshops, seminars, books, and periodicals been focused on the theme of awakening to our inner spirit. There is a resurgence of interest in angels to the point that it is not possible to go anywhere without seeing them featured on TV, in books, on clothes, statues, figurines, bedding, and even on the covers of the most conservative news magazines. The scientific community is intensely studying the healing power of faith, love, and prayer. Major efforts are being made to revitalize and recycle our earth's resources. And people are taking responsibility to actively participate in their own healing processes as evidenced by the widespread acceptance of natural, alternative health care. Another unusual trend is occurring—whether practical or not, people are leaving well-paid, traditional jobs to respond to an intuitive calling to find careers in which they can express their inner truth. We are realizing that making a living is not the same thing as making a life, as indicated by the increasing numbers of people who are placing a higher priority on fulfillment and simplicity of lifestyle than on monetary wealth.

What Is Happening? What Has Changed?

We have! There is a world not only outside of us but within us as well—what we are seeing in our outer existence is a direct reflection of what is happening within our personal lives. The social changes we are experiencing are not issues in themselves, but evidence of a major shift in our thinking— we are moving away from the external values of materialism and moving toward the human inner values of spirit.

After centuries of looking to our outer world for our sustenance and power, we are remembering a place deep within our souls where we have limitless access to unconditional love, support, renewal, and inspiration. Our soul is our connection to spirit, and it is within this space that we have a sense of correctness that is our truth. As we get in touch with our inner truth, we are coming to realize that many aspects of our personal lives do not coincide with our inner values. If our personal lives are not reflecting our truth, then the external social institutions which we have created in this frame of mind do not reflect our truth. Since many things in our lives are changing at the same time, we may feel that we have lost the points of reference which, in the past, have kept us centered.

The brilliant ray of light shining through all of this confusion is that the chaos we are experiencing is a burst of energy giving rise to a more enlightened society that is redefining the center of its existence to coincide with the integrity of spirit. We are becoming aware that we need to find our security internally rather than in external institutions. Instead of looking to our outer world to define and control us, we are taking personal responsibility to turn to our inner spirit to reveal who we are and why we are here. Our souls are uniting in a common desire to create a new sense of world order which resonates with the truth that resides within the deepest level of our being. This desire is for a sense of order within our minds, not just in the conditions around us. We are longing for a life of self-respect and peace and are becoming mindful of the fact that these qualities are a reflection of our internal state of being, not of external conditions. We are yearning to reclaim our sense of self and our passion for life, and we are realizing these are things that can be found only inside of our hearts and minds, not in a material world outside of ourselves.

What we are witnessing is a healthy reflection of humanity's spiritual growth as, one by one, we are being called upon to heal our world by healing our personal lives.

Where Do We Begin in Our Healing?

The first step in all healing begins at the level of self and the awareness that change is necessary. The time has come for us to change a perception we have collectively adopted of seeing ourselves as victims of our environment. This is a disabling perception which makes us feel very angry with the things "they" are doing to "us."

Yet, can we truly believe that each one of us has not played some part in creating the world we are seeing? Our outer existence is a summary of our collective personal inner values. The very social institutions that we feel are failing us are merely mirror images of the society that built them. We are the people who own the companies, manage the companies, work in the companies, elect the government officials, are the government officials, choose the medical professionals, are the medical professionals, teach the students, are the students, lead the religions, follow the religions, and are the members of our own families. We have magnified our thoughts in grandiose measure by constructing social institutions which echo our personal values. Why do we seek to blame? If we insist on thinking there is an enemy, perhaps we need to consider what the cartoon character Pogo said, "We have met the enemy, and he is us!"

The external confusion we are experiencing in our homes, at work, in school, and all around us is not some form of divine punishment. This idea comes from a perception which assumes we are at the mercy of a physical world that happened to us. As humanity matures, we are coming to realize that our physical circumstances do not create our thoughts—it is the other way around. The world we are seeing with our physical eyes is what we have created together through the collective energy of our thoughts and actions. Just as our personal states of ease and dis-ease register within our individual bodies, our collective state of health is reflected in the body of our outer world. The crime, violence, diseases, poverty, and general social upheaval which we are witnessing are all symptoms of our societal pain. It is critical to the welfare of humanity that we release our victim perspective and embrace the truth:

We can only change the quality of our collective present reality by taking personal responsibility for the part we have each played in creating it. All change begins at the level of self. As we change our individual lives, the world around us changes as well.

The crisis we are experiencing is an extremely encouraging indication. We are not accepting what we are seeing in our outer world because it no longer coincides with our inner beliefs about what feels correct at a soul level. What we are seeing is what we have thus far created together, largely in an unconscious way, through our thoughts and actions. We are moving toward a far more enlightened space of creating a reality, in a *conscious* way, that reflects the whole of who we truly are.

We can perceive this crisis as social destruction and random confusion. On the other hand, we can choose to see our world in a new light. Indeed, the word *crisis*, defined by Webster as *a turning point for the better or worse*, is derived from the Greek root word, *krisis*, which literally means *decision.* We can decide to make this a turning point for the better by making a commitment to our own personal healing.

While it is apparent that our spiritual consciousness is awakening, change is only possible when we are committed to act upon our awareness. Each of us has a sacred mission to play an active role in the healing of our earth, starting with our own lives. Throughout these pages we will focus on how our individual spiritual healing influences the consciousness of our entire planet.

Part One

Remembering Our Spiritual Truth

Chapter One

The Nature of Our Whole Self

We begin to realize our extraordinary human potential to participate in creating a better world by remembering that not only do we exist in this physical world of matter we call earth—we also concurrently exist in a metaphysical (beyond the physical) non-material world.

Because we exist in both the material and non-material realms, our *whole self* is both physical mass and energy. Like water and ice, mass and energy are just different aspects of the same thing.

What Is Our "Whole Self?"

Our whole self is our body, mind, and spirit.

Our bodies and minds function in our material (physical) world and our spirit functions in the non-material (spiritual) world of pure energy. Although each aspect of our existence is expressed in a different way, we can and do function at all levels concurrently. Every time we dream we are demonstrating our ability to physically reside in our bodies at the same time we are using our minds to access the subconscious level of our spirit and we can be anywhere at any time.

We will be discussing the nature of our whole self in detail; for now let's begin by taking a general look at the nature of the different aspects of our existence:

Spirit—Our Spirit, also known as our Essential Self, exists in the non-material, non-tangible realm of our existence, which is pure energy. *Essence*, the root word of essential, means the fundamental nature or quality of something.

Our Essential Self is who we are in the truest and purest sense and is our intuitive connection to all of creation and universal love. This is the space where, at a subconscious level, we already know all that we need to know because we are all a part of universal intelligence.

Mind—Our minds consciously sense and interpret the wisdom of spirit through various ways, such as meditation, intuitive feelings, dreams, imagination, and visions.

Body—Our bodies exist on the material plane of our existence and are the tangible, most evident aspect of ourselves. This is the physical aspect of our being with which we are most familiar. Our bodies are the visible embodiment of our mind and spirit.

In order to get in touch with our inner truth, it is imperative that we remember that our whole self is the integration of these three aspects. As we work to understand our true nature, we see the importance of both the material and non-material realms of our existence.

What Is a Material World?

Our material world is a world of matter which can be perceived physically by one or more of our five senses—sight, sound, touch, taste, and smell. We sense our physical world as objective, solid, and three dimensional. Most of our attention is focused on our physical world because it is a tangible world that is readily accessed by one or all of our five senses. Of the five senses which we have been given to interpret our world, we take in the greatest amount of information through sight, so we tend to believe that the only "real world" is the one we can see with our physical eyes.

Our modern society uses science as the ultimate authority to validate what is "real" to us in this material, physical world, and it is through the realm of science that we gain the knowledge that helps us to begin to understand the vastness, power, and mystery of our universe; however, if we base our world view of all that exists exclusively on scientific justification, are we attempting to squash the truth of the universe to fit within the confines of our knowledge?

In many ways, our scientific mind set has preempted our intuition and faith in the unknown in that many of us believe that unless something can be scientifically proven, it does not exist. Nevertheless, at a deeper heart level we can sense the truth of existence of many things which cannot be scientifically proven, such as love. In the 1997 movie "Contact," a spiritual guru asked a scientist to validate scientifically that she loved her deceased father, something she was unable to do; and yet the majority of us have sensed the "unprovable" love of another person.

If we stay within the boundaries of accepting as reality only that which is presently deemed as scientific truth, do we also close our minds to the existence of experiences that transcend logical explanation, such as spontaneous healing?

This was an issue which came to my mind when I was working with Carl, a client who was diagnosed with an advanced case of lung cancer. When I first met Carl, he had just been told by his physician that, based on his bleak medical test results, he had approximately five months to live. Rather than waiting to see what might happen, Carl told me he wanted to be proactive about his health and asked if I would help him. He readily embraced the concept of holistic health and diligently committed himself to participating in holistic healing sessions and practicing many natural healing processes. Three months after we began, Carl returned to his physician for a check-up. To the amazement of his physician, all the medical tests indicated that the malignant spots had disappeared and that the formerly diseased lung was completely healthy. There was no indication of cancer anywhere in his body. The doctor, when faced with Carl's mysterious recovery and enthusiasm, was agitated and insisted that Carl accept the "reality" that the cancer would most likely return since his recovery could not be medically justified. Carl was surprised to find himself in the position of actually pleading with his doctor to at least consider the possibility that he was healed. He agreed to have periodic checkups but chose to hold to his belief that the miraculous healing he was experiencing, although not logically explainable, was possible. More than six years have gone by, Carl is still healthy and free of cancer, and his former doctor is still holding out on whether or not to acknowledge the truth of his recovery.

Although it is understandable that Carl's physician felt professionally compelled to point out the risk of a recurrence, the point of this true story is that we can get so locked into our paradigms of having to justify things scientifically that we run the risk of denying the evidence of miraculous events just because we cannot explain them.

As humanity evolves, we are beginning to open our minds to infinitely greater possibilities than we are perceiving with our physical senses and logical theories. We are remembering that we are also a part of a reality which transcends our physical world.

Albert Einstein, one of the greatest scientists of the last century, bridged the physical and non-physical worlds in the early 1900's with his Theory of Relativity, $e = mc^2$, which introduced the concept that all matter is also energy. Indeed, his theory is commonly accepted by present-day physicists. The Theory of Relativity opens our minds to a much broader dimension of thinking that embraces the concept that everything within our world, organic and non-organic, is energy. **From this perspective, we are not only material beings living in our physical world but also non-material beings of energy living in a non-material world!**

What Is a Non-Material World?

The non-material world, also known as the meta-physical, spiritual world, is beyond the realm of time, space, and matter. It is not tangible because it transcends the limitation of our five senses. It is an invisible, universal, collective field of energy with properties that our conscious mind cannot grasp within the context of words and logic. This is because the infinite quality of nature expands beyond our present perceptions and scientific paradigms.

What Is Energy?

Energy is defined by Webster as *inherent power, capacity for action.* In physics, energy is defined as *the capacity for doing work.* Whether we define energy literally or scientifically, we see that it is the capacity to create, not something which is concrete and material within itself. Quantum theory shows us that, in addition to being a *universal field*, some of the characteristics of energy are that it is *formless, unlimited, infinite potential, and is in constant motion.*

Realizing that we are energy helps us to understand that our human potential far surpasses the limitations of our physical state of being!

Let's take a closer look at the characteristics of energy and how they apply to our innate human nature:

Universal Field

There is a common bond of energy that interconnects us with each other and with all of nature, also known as a universal field. The energy within Americans is the same energy as within every other human being in every other country in the world. The energy within humanity is the same that is within the flowers, trees, animals, wind, oceans, stars, sun, moon, and all that exists, and the energy within all these things is a part of the energy of all that is. In much of Asia, this energy is commonly known as *prana* or *chi.*

The universal field is the energy of life—it is our spiritual connection with the universe. The word *spirit* is from the Latin root word, *spiritus*, which means *life force, breath.* In essence, the universal field is the unified spirit from which we all draw breath!

Formless

Energy has no definite shape or form; therefore, we are not bound by our perceptions of the limitations of linear measurement of time and space. When we look at ourselves from this aspect, we are far more expansive than our physical bodies because there are no boundaries on our energy. The energy of our spirit, unlike our bodies, can be anywhere at the same time. For example, when we are driving, our spirit can be in our physical bodies in the car at the same time that we can be present, although not physically, with anyone at any location.

Unlimited

The universal field of energy is a life force which is always available—we cannot create or destroy it. The amount of energy we can receive is unlimited, and we have as much access to the flow of energy as we are willing to receive.

Huge amounts of energy can result from a tiny amount of mass when matter is completely converted to energy. Einstein's Theory of Relativity indicates that the energy equivalent of one gram of mass (i.e. approximately 15.5 grains of wheat) could produce about 25 million kilowatt hours of electricity. According to the *World Book Encyclopedia*, 25 million kilowatt hours is enough electricity to keep a 100-watt bulb burning for more than 28,500 years!

When we look at the universal field as the source of all energy, we become aware that we all have access to an endless power supply. In fact, every time we inhale, we are taking in universal spiritual energy. Since the energy comes through us, not from us, we can tap this limitless source for ourselves at any time and anywhere.

Because we all have direct access to this energy source, we do not need to take energy away from other people. For example, a glass of water can be refilled by putting the glass under the faucet or by pouring it from someone else's glass. If we have access to a common source for water, why take it from someone else?

Infinite Potential

The universal field is a field of collective intelligence which holds infinite potential and is available to all of us. It expresses itself through the channels of our minds in the energy of our thoughts.

It is within this non-material field of energy that we humans have an inherent ability to access universal truth and wisdom through our intuition, dreams, and imagination.

The universal field is the source of all material creation—whatever we can perceive with our minds can be created in our physical world. In fact, everything that exists in our material world began with the pure energy of someone's thoughts and ideas.

Constant Motion

Energy, by its very definition, is continuous movement. It cannot stand still and must move in a constant motion called *vibration.*

As humans, we also are vibrations of energy. When we see ourselves as vibrations of energy, we realize that our lives are not a static condition but a process of constant change, growth, and evolution.

Every cell within our bodies is constantly changing with the flow of energy—in fact, scientific studies have proven that our cells change so rapidly that we have an entirely new body every few years! This tells us that we are not reservoirs storing energy. We are channels of a constant flow of unlimited energy—therefore, we are in constant motion!

If We Cannot Perceive Energy with Our Five Senses, How Do We Know That It Exists?

We know that energy exists in the elements of nature because we can harness it for our physical use. We harness the energy of the sun through solar cells; the wind with windmills; water through waterfalls, hydro-electric water wheels and dams; nuclear material with reactors; and organic matter with natural and chemical processes that convert it into fuels. These forms of energy are not tangible; nonetheless, we can certainly feel the effects of their existence each day of our lives. Every time we pay our electric bill, we are acknowledging the reality of something we cannot touch, see, hear, smell, or taste—yet we certainly are aware of when we have electricity and when we don't.

We Can Sense Energy Outside of Our Bodies

All of nature is energy. Is there anything more energizing and regenerating than inhaling fresh air, looking at beautiful flowers, standing in a lush green meadow, feeling the warmth of the sun on our face as we listen to the mesmerizing sound of ocean waves, walking in the woods on a crisp autumn day, or gazing at the awesome beauty of a mountain?

We humans seem to have a built-in energy sensor with which we can instantly detect the collective energy of our surroundings without any logical explanation. Our sense of the nature of the energy outside of us varies with the situation. We even use terms to describe this sensation, such as "good vibes" and "bad vibes," which describe our energetic impressions of the vibrations of people and situations, based solely on our intuitive senses.

For example, when we enter a nursery school and see vibrant children laughing and playing we may sense that we are enveloped by light, uplifting energy. For those of us who like sports, think of how charged up we feel by the excitement of the energy around us when we walk into a football stadium when the home team has just scored a touchdown!

On the other hand, if we walk into a business conference room in which a group of people have just had an oppressive meeting about downsizing and lay-offs, most of us would instantly feel heavy, depressing energy even after everyone had left the room. Chances are that we would sense frenetic, scattered energy walking into the emergency room of a hospital.

The capacity to sense external energies, both positive and negative, comes naturally to all of us.

We Can Sense Energy Within Our Bodies

Nature's flow of energy is always available to us—the degree to which we are open to it depends upon our emotional balance. When we are emotionally at ease, energy freely flows through our bodies, causing us to sense an expansion of ourselves. When we feel emotional disease, energy flows less freely, and we sense a contraction of ourselves.

One of the most dramatic examples of sensing the expansiveness of energy within our bodies is the state of being in love. When we are in love, we feel creative, open, alive, whole, unlimited, and elevated. Not only do we feel uplifted, we feel like everyone around us is as well. We are in synch with the flow of life. The blissful state of being in love gives us a taste of being totally open and "at one" with the energy of the Universe.

Conversely, when we are feeling emotional stress, such as being angry, depressed, or guilty, we sense our energy is blocked by our negative emotions—we actually feel contracted, as though our world is coming in on us. Our bodies visibly reflect this contracted state by feeling tight and shut down. The phrase, "Sit down, I have bad news," is an expression which supports the fact that when we are shocked or sad, we literally experience a block of energy in our muscles that causes us to collapse. When we are angry or frightened, we may sense the contraction of our energy through headaches, a taut neck, tight shoulders, a backache, stomach pain, weak knees, or clammy hands. As with external energy, all of us innately have the capacity to sense and experience different energies within our bodies.

We Can Sense the Energy of Other People

We can also pick up on the energy of others. When we are around people who have a positive attitude about life, who accept us for who we are and encourage us, we feel uplifted and revitalized. On the other hand, sharing company with people who have a negative attitude about life or who criticize and try to control us can cause us to feel contracted and drained as though our energy flow is being suffocated.

The point to all of these examples is that although energy is not perceivable to any of our five senses, all forms of nature, including our bodies, validate the existence of it every moment of every day.

What Is The Importance of Recognizing We Are Energy?

We've always been aware that our bodies are part of the material, physical world. While this is true, when we perceive ourselves exclusively as matter, we are only acknowledging the body/mind aspects of ourselves. This perspective completely ignores the non-material world where the infinite potential of our spirit exists. When we remember that we exist in both the material and non-material dimensions we are acknowledging our whole self.

Chapter Two

We Create Our Reality

When we see our whole self—body, mind, and spirit—from the integrated perspective of both our physical and metaphysical existence, we begin to recognize our true human nature. We are more than just our bodies and minds—the spiritual aspect of our being is *formless, unlimited, infinite potential, constant motion, and part of a universal field of energy.*

Realizing that we are energy, as well as matter, opens our awareness to our extraordinary human potential. Energy is the capacity to create; therefore, **we are dynamic, creative beings.** We express our human creative nature spiritually, mentally, and physically in the following ways:

Spirit - Our spirit expresses its creative nature through the pure energy of thought.

Mind - Our mind expresses our thoughts through the energy of the words and actions we choose.

Body - Our body expresses our creative nature through the experiences which result from the thoughts, words, and actions we choose.

Because we are creative beings, it is extremely important to become aware of how the energy of our thoughts, words, and actions shapes our personal and collective realities.

What Is Personal Reality?

Our personal reality (inner world) is our individual experience of the world we create for ourselves, based on our thoughts. Even though there are millions of events going on all around us at any given time, the only reality of which we are aware are the events that occur in our own personal lives. If we want to take stock of how we have been thinking over the years, we need only to look at our lives—our relationships, health, careers, and financial situation are all manifestations of our past thoughts, which have become our personal reality.

This is why our thoughts are so powerful. Once we understand that we can choose our thoughts, we can no longer perceive our thinking as an involuntary action and our lives as something that happens to us. When we consciously choose our thoughts and how we express them, we are taking responsibility for the quality of our lives. Rather than think of ourselves as being beholden to our outer world, we see the truth of our role in helping to create it. This is an awesome realization because it means **we can create a new personal reality simply by changing the way in which we choose to think!**

What Is Our Collective Reality?

Our collective reality (outer world) is the sum of the personal realities of all of us. The condition of our world is like a gigantic mirror reflecting back to us the result of the thoughts which humanity, as a whole, is choosing.

If the collective reality we see in our outer world includes crime, violence, greed, and disharmony, this is a very definite indication that we each have to work on changing our inner personal realities. We can change the collective reality of our outer world by taking responsibility for the thoughts we are choosing that are creating the reality of our inner, personal world.

Why Are Our Thoughts So Powerful?

Whether or not we are conscious of it, our minds are always working. Every thought we have is an energetic impulse which is constantly creating who we are and the circumstances within our lives. Our thoughts determine our perception of who we are. For example, if we think we are successful, we are correct. If we think we are not successful, we are also correct. In the words of Buddha, "You are what you think. All that you are arises with your thoughts. With your thoughts you make your world."

We are each participating in the awesome process of creation with each thought that we have. Creation is not only something which has already happened—it is the eternal moment-to-moment manifestations of the energy of our thinking. Even though we tend to think of only certain types of people as "creative people," such as painters, sculptors, and dancers, the truth is that every human being is creative because everyone has thoughts! In the spiritual sense, we are all painters creating a picture of our personal reality with the brush of every thought; we are all sculptors molding our perceptions into physical form; and we are all dancers synchronizing our physical movement with the vibration of our thinking.

The creative dynamic of thought is sometimes referred to as The Law of Manifestation. *Manifestation* is the process of our thoughts becoming evident to one or more of our five physical senses. Like gravity, manifestation is a principle of nature which is constantly in effect whether we are aware of it or not. We begin to appreciate the awesome power of our thoughts by understanding some of the dynamics of the principle of manifestation:

- All of our thoughts manifest into our physical world;
- What we focus on expands;
- What we think is what we attract; and
- We can change our reality by changing our thoughts.

All of Our Thoughts Manifest into Our Physical World

Energy is an amoeba-like field of potential all around us. Just as we can only utilize the energy of the sun, wind, water, and earth by harnessing it, we can only realize the creative power of our energy by consciously focusing our thoughts. Focusing has a laser-like intensity which manifests our thought processes into physical form.

Everything we see and experience in our physical world began as a thought. Whether it be the chair on which we are sitting or the wedding reception we are attending this weekend, it all began as an idea in someone's mind. We are always thinking, whether we are aware of it or not; therefore, we are perpetually creating. Until we are aware of what we are thinking, we remain unconscious of what the energy of our thoughts is producing. Our thoughts, both positive and negative, generate our reality. Hatred and violence are manifestations of our negative thoughts, just as love and peace are manifestations of our positive thoughts. The question is: Do we want to create *consciously* from the spiritual space of our inner truth, or do we want to unconsciously allow the energy of mass consciousness to govern our thoughts? Living a life of integrity requires that we master our own thought processes rather than allowing our thoughts to be controlled by others or trying to control the thoughts of others.

Once we become aware of our power to create, we begin to realize that it is of paramount importance that we be mindful of the intention with which we project the energy of our thoughts. *Intention* is more than just words—it is the objective of our thoughts underlying our words and actions.

We are all channels of universal energy which is consistently flowing through us. Because universal energy is the essence of life, it is neutral; however, as it flows through our minds it becomes positive or negative energy, based on our intentions.

If we say, "My, don't you look special today," with kind intention, we are expressing positive energy.

If we make that same exact statement with an intention of criticism, we are expressing negative energy. The energy of what we have projected then registers as physical reality in terms of how the people around us receive the energy of our thoughts.

Thinking with kind intention does not just happen. It is a conscious choice that becomes a habit. Like all habits, the more we practice it, the stronger it becomes.

What We Focus on Expands

When we steadfastly hold to an intention, whatever we are concentrating on expands, whether it is a person or a situation. For example, when we consciously intend to concentrate on what we like about someone, we find more to like about that person; when our intention is to concentrate on their faults, we increasingly find more to dislike about that person. The following exercise demonstrates this principle:

Think of someone, anyone, whom you know. Set the intention in your mind to focus on everything that you respect and like about him or her. You don't need to say a thing, just channel your thinking to focus on their likeable qualities. Take note of this person's reaction to you the next time you see them. You will probably notice that every quality you are concentrating on becomes apparent to you when you are in this person's presence. Did the person change, or did you just change your focus?

Anyone who has been in sales is probably very aware of how our focus expands our reality. When numerous consecutive sales calls do not materialize into closures, we may feel like we are on a sinking ship. Even though we are making the same effort, nothing seems to work so we tend to feel rejected on every sales call we make. Yet, all it takes is one sale to change our "luck" and suddenly we experience a series of successful closures. Is this because our luck changes or because we change our focus from failure to success?

What We Think is What We Attract

When we set our thoughts into motion with our intentions, the universe responds through the law of attraction. Because every thought is an electrical impulse each of us is like a TV station in that we transmit our thoughts by sending out a certain frequency. The frequencies of our thoughts are *vibrations*. The vibrations of our thoughts magnetize other thoughts on the same frequency, so whatever we send out is what comes back to us; i.e. thoughts of love attract love and thoughts of fear attract fear.

For example, when we focus our thoughts on everything that is right about our lives, we send out a frequency that attracts people and circumstances that support our positive thoughts, thereby confirming our attitude that life is a wonderful adventure. When we transmit thoughts which focus on all the bad things that can happen to us, we are sending out a frequency which attracts people and circumstances that resonate with our thoughts of fear, confirming our thoughts that life is a frightening experience.

As we each become increasingly aware of our whole self, our human race is escalating to a higher, faster vibrational level which responds more readily to the esoteric, subtle energies of healing intention.

We Can Change Our Reality
by Changing Our Thoughts

If we don't like what we see in our exterior world, we don't have to wait for the circumstances to change. We have the creative power to change our external circumstances by changing the interior world of our thoughts!

How many times have we heard ourselves and others say that our lives will be better when we have more money, more time, less work, fewer problems, and the list goes on and on. We are, in essence, waiting for our circumstances to change us instead of changing our situations by changing our thoughts. Our life circumstances are not the cause of our thoughts—they are the result of the thoughts we are sending out to the world! We do not need to wait for our circumstances to change before we feel better. **When we choose to think differently the circumstances will follow our thoughts.**

Life is not a permanent condition. It is a dynamic process of constant change and growth. If we don't like what we are attracting, we can change the thoughts we are projecting. Our frequency then changes, as does everything we attract. The frequency at which we are projecting our thoughts is what determines the nature of our personal reality.

Is It Really Possible to Change Our Personal Reality by Changing Our Thoughts?

It is a universal truth that every time we change our thoughts, we change our reality. In fact, the ideal times to practice this are when we are encountering major challenges. When we are in a crisis of any kind, we become paralyzed if we continue to focus on everything that is "happening to us" instead of choosing thoughts which focus on a new reality. If we continue to think about how bad our external conditions are rather than choosing to focus on more constructive thoughts, the chances are that we will continue to repeat the same unhealthy patterns of conduct. This explains how we can be in an emotionally destructive situation and get caught in an endless loop of experiencing different versions of the same theme. For example, how many of us have had a string of unhappy dating relationships only to discover that all of the people we are attracting to us represent the same emotional issues with different faces? If we continue to weave our lives with self-defeating thoughts, eventually we become totally ensnared in our own emotional web.

When we wait for our outer reality to change our inner reality, we are delegating our inner power to create our personal reality to everyone other than ourselves, causing us to feel that we have no control over our lives.

Understanding how our thoughts form the perceptions that shape our reality is the foundation of our personal healing process.

What Are Perceptions?

Perception is how we interpret our environment through physical sensation. One way to envision our individual perceptions is to imagine that we are all born with our own personal paint brush and a palette with a rainbow of colors. Our life is the neutral canvas on which each of us paints our own individual pictures of how we see our experiences. One person's picture may be delicate brushes with a few objects of pastel colors, another a very busy picture in broad strokes of vivid colors, yet another in all different shades of the same color with no objects at all.

The greatest divine gift given to humanity is free will to choose our personal perceptions.

Will is defined by Webster as, *to determine by an act of choice; the mental powers manifested as wishing, choosing, desiring, or intending.* When we are aware that we can choose our perceptions, we empower ourselves to live consciously. If we are not aware of our inner power to make choices, we live our lives unconsciously.

Whether we are conscious of it or not, our perceptions determine the way in which we see and experience absolutely everything in our lives. While we may all be looking at the same scenery, each person's picture is different because we all sense life in a unique and individual way. This is why we can all experience the same thing, yet have entirely different responses. It also explains why ten people can interpret the same situation in ten different ways, each one thinking that he or she is right. It does not matter how anyone else sees the scenery, the individual pictures we perceive with our minds are what is real for each of us. In essence, each of us is an artist painting our own personal reality through our unique perceptions.

If We Can Change Our Reality
with the Conscious Choice of Our Thoughts,
Why Don't We Just Change Our Thinking?

The willingness of each of us to recognize our infinite potential to create depends on the beliefs which we, and the generations that preceded us, have developed throughout the years. Many of us have forgotten our inner power because we believe that our lives are a permanent condition created by someone else. There is a certain measure of pseudo-security in this point of view because we can somewhat hide from life by blaming others for the circumstances we experience.

Awakening to the truth of our inner power to create means we have to take responsibility for how our thoughts are creating our personal reality. As we become aware of the creative power of our thoughts, we can empower ourselves to choose perceptions of life which coincide with our inner truth.

Even If We Are Willing to Take Responsibility for
Our Choice of Perceptions, Aren't There Certain
Conditions in Life over Which We Have No
Human Control?

Although we can always choose how we want to *perceive* a situation, there are many things in life over which we have no control. We all live under certain universal principles of organization which are not subject to our human decisions. We do not get to personally choose such things as what time the sun comes up in the morning, when the seasons change, or when and where lightening strikes because the coordination and synchronism of the energy of nature is a divine master plan which is part of a reality far greater than our human physical world.

Because we are all a part of this divine master plan, many of the things we need to benefit the growth of our soul may be out of our conscious control; such as, when we are born, who our family members are, the genetic coding determining our personal characteristics, and when and how we die.

What *choice* means is that even though we cannot control everything that happens in our lives, each of us is responsible for choosing how we want to interpret and respond to life events and situations. If we change one letter in the spelling of the word responsible—to respons-*able*—we are reminded that we are all *able* to choose our *responses* to life.

We can wake up in the morning and choose to savor the warmth of the sun on our faces, and stretch our bodies in eager anticipation of the day; we can also awaken and choose to recoil from the sunlight, pull the cover over our heads, and postpone facing the day as long as possible. While it is not our personal choice to decide whether the world will see a new day or not, *how* we personally experience it is totally a matter of how we choose to respond.

There are no right or wrong perceptions. We are all on this same wonderful journey of self-discovery called life. Being here on earth is divine plan—the nature and quality of our life adventure is a matter of choice. Our personal perceptions determine what paths we take, the speed with which we learn and grow, the nature of our experiences, and how much we may enjoy the process of moving toward our spiritual truth.

The quality of our lives does not depend on the actual events we experience; rather it depends on how we interpret them. There are positive and negative opportunities for growth in every situation we encounter and through everyone whom we meet—we can decide which way we want to slant our focus. For example, most of us think of winning the lottery as a positive event that would automatically bring us great happiness. For some, it has—yet for many it has been perceived as the cause of great unhappiness in the form of alienated relationships with friends and family members, loss of privacy, constant harassment from people seeking donations, lots of calls from financial advisers, and the pressure of making prudent decisions on where and how to spend large amounts of money.

On the other hand, one of the most deplorable events in human history, the Holocaust, has been perceived in a constructive way through the eyes of many enlightened survivors who have shared inspiring stories relating how they have been able to sense light and life purpose in the midst of enormous darkness and misery.

As we become aware of what our perceptions are and our inner power to choose them, we empower ourselves to expand them to align with broader perspectives which incorporate a larger world view.

What Is Perspective?

Perspective is the overall viewpoint from which we see the world. Our perspectives are the context and our perceptions are the content. For example, when we imagine a glass filled with water, we can relate the glass to the context and the water to the content. Similarly, if we use the analogy of an artist painting a picture of his personal reality, perspective is the frame and perception is the picture.

We don't actually see our perspectives. We look at life through our perspectives, much the same as we see through our eyeglasses. It is like cutting a tiny slit into a box and putting the box over our heads. If we look through the slit, all we can see is a narrow perspective of a much larger view, and yet we may think it is all there is to see.

Perspectives are self-imposed mental boundaries (also known as paradigms) that can blind us from seeing larger possibilities. For example, many perspectives which have been perceived as the end of the rainbow in the past have been totally blown away by broader present-day thinking, as is evident in the following actual quotes:

"Everything that can be invented has been invented."
—Director of the U.S. Patent Office in 1899

"Groups with guitars are on the way out."
—Decca Records turning down the Beatles in 1962

"There is no reason to have a computer in your home."
—President of Digital Equipment in 1977

As we can see by the above examples, perspectives expand as we grow. When we look at some of the basic stages of our personal physical growth, we can see this more clearly, as follows:

— Perspectives During Our Physical Growth —

Infancy—When we are babies, we have a very near-sighted outlook because we are focused on survival instincts. During this stage we are very aware of our bodies; and for a while, our mothers and food are our entire world. When we start to crawl, our world expands to a myopic view of our physical reality, such as the dust on the floor and a paper clip that someone has dropped.

Childhood—As we grow into childhood, our world expands as we begin to develop an ego and sense of individuality. During this stage of growth, we become more aware of the mental level of our existence, and we like to remind our parents that we have a mind of our own by frequently taking an opposite point of view (oh, the infamous two's!). Our perspective begins to widen as we begin to walk and see that there is a world outside of us.

Adolescence—When we grow into adolescence, our world continues to broaden as we explore the relationship of self with our outer world. Not only can we walk, we can see a great deal more of the world by driving in a car, taking a train or bus, or flying in a plane. During this stage, we are aware of the connection between the mental and physical aspects of ourselves. This is the typical teen-age stage of experimenting with many different ways of communicating and expressing ourselves as part of our self-discovery process of seeing how we fit into the larger scheme of things.

Maturity—When we are willing to move into maturity, our world expands even more as we begin to realize that our minds and bodies are a part of our inner spirit, and our individual spirit is connected to one universal spirit. From this perspective, we are able to rise above our physical reality and see the much larger picture of life. It is a bit like having an aerial view while standing on top of a mountain and being able to observe how people are driving in cars, working in their jobs, birds are singing, the wind is blowing, and flowers are blooming all at the same time. While on one hand each is functioning separately, they are all a part of a synchronous whole functioning simultaneously and governed by an organized holistic energy.

We individually experience these stages of broadening our perspectives not only physically, but also spiritually in the form of our emotional development. Just because we are in the adult phase of *physical* growth does not necessarily mean we have reached *emotional* maturity. We can be fifty years old, physically mature, and remain emotionally locked into perceptions of life framed around the childhood perspective of building our ego and proving our individuality to the world. Conversely, many of us have met young children who seem to have the spiritual maturity of an ancient soul. As our individual spiritual awareness grows, our collective world perspective is expanding.

How Is Our Collective World Perspective Expanding?

Just as our individual perspectives grow, so also does our collective world perspective. There was a time in history when our world view was that the earth was flat and the center of all that existed, and most of our personal perceptions revolved around this paradigm. Through scientific exploration we have continued to expand our collective world view to embrace new perspectives—not only is our earth round, but our planet is only a part of an infinitely larger universe, which is part of an even greater whole. The more we learn about ourselves, the larger our perspective becomes.

In the words of the late Carl Sagan, renowned astronomer/scientist, "Getting to the moon was perhaps not as important as seeing ourselves from it."

Our world society is not only expanding its collective perspective of the physical world—we are also seeing evidence of our collective emotional and spiritual growth. The social upheaval we are experiencing is an indication that our global society is growing beyond the limited perspectives of physical survival and the ego gratification of materialism. We are moving toward the much more evolved and expansive perspective of recognizing that we are citizens of an interconnected global community.

Our society is making a major paradigm shift from a life theme of living from the *outside-in*, a perspective based on surviving our outer physical world, to the more expanded perspective of living from the *inside-out*, a life theme based on the values of our inner spirit.

As we take a closer look at these perspectives, we can see that the "outside-in" approach focuses on a Perspective of Separation which views our bodies and minds as separate from our spirit, whereas the "inside-out" approach is a Perspective of Oneness which embraces not only the body and mind aspects of ourselves that exist in our material world, but also the spiritual aspect of our whole self which exists in our non-material world.

The Perspective of Separation is our traditional paradigm of thinking. Each of us must explore how we have lived in this limiting perspective in the past in order to heal and expand to broader, more expansive perspectives that are aligned with our spiritual truth.

Chapter Three

The Perspective of Separation

The Perspective of Separation is a view of life in which we see our concrete, physical world as our only reality. This is a model of life in which we live from the *outside-in* because we look to our outer physical world for our energy and verification of self-worth rather than living from the core of our inner spirit. Up to this point in time, it has been the predominant theme for our personal lives and social structures, particularly in the Western Hemisphere.

The Perspective of Separation is based on fear and perpetuates an existence based on competition and survival because it emphasizes the parts rather than the whole of our existence. It is a view of life which focuses on separation within and without in that we view our material world as separate and disconnected from the non-material world of spirit, perceive our own lives as separate and disconnected from the lives of each other, and perceive the inner makeup of our own minds and bodies as being separate from our spirit.

Because this perspective of life does not acknowledge the connection of our minds and bodies with the limitless life energy within the non-material world of spirit, we look to each other to replenish our energy and to prove our individual supremacy. Accordingly, the outside-in perspective is based on external control and hierarchy. It is very important that we understand this perspective which focuses on separation because, just as the contrast of darkness enables us to know light, it is by understanding the parts of who we are that we can embrace the larger meaning of life.

How Does The Perspective of Separation
Help Us Embrace the Larger Meaning of Life?

Experiencing life from the Perspective of Separation is vital to our human evolution because we can only embrace the larger concept of "we" by first understanding who "me" is. In other words, in order to see all of life in a holistic, interconnected way, we have to first experience the fractionated perspectives of all the parts of ourselves. Like a puzzle, we can only appreciate the awesome beauty of the whole of life through the joy of seeing how all the pieces fit together.

Our physical world provides infinite opportunities to explore every aspect of our true nature. It is a world of polarity in that everything within our material existence has an opposing extreme. It is here that we experience life and death, light and dark, male and female, electrical and magnetic, good and bad, left and right, up and down, in and out, all or nothing, and hot and cold. Our material world is the perfect classroom in which to discover our individual uniqueness and the world around us through the process of relativity. How would we know happiness without knowing sadness? Good without knowing bad? And light without knowing darkness? How could we even comprehend what balance means without experiencing both ends of the spectrum?

Because our material world is so amazingly diversified, it offers us a vast arena in which to exercise our free will to make choices. If we had no options, everything in our lives would be neutral, and we would not be able to explore our human nature. In fact, we can only realize what neutral is by knowing both polarities. And if we did not have the opportunity to experience how the energy of our thoughts, words, and actions manifest into physical form, we would not realize how our choices create our reality. It is through struggling with these dynamic opposites that we gain a better understanding of who we are and why we are here. Understanding the whole of life is not something which we are simply given—we have to *earn* our understanding by working our way through the many challenges that exist within our world of polarity.

What Does Living from the "Outside-In" Mean?

Living from the outside-in is a model of life that has evolved from our collective Perspective of Separation and is based on materialism and personal ego. When we live from the outside-in, we mold the purpose of our lives to fit within the context of expectations from our outer physical world because the material world is the only dimension of our existence which we acknowledge.

When we live this model of life, we delegate the responsibility for our regeneration of energy, personal growth, and self-identity to outside sources, such as employers, religious organizations, educational institutions, medical professionals, government organizations, and perhaps even spouses, friends and relatives. If we believe that our well-being and self-worth depend entirely on outside approval, we have to design our behavior to elicit praise, support, money, power or whatever we feel we need from these external sources. In essence, we allow other people and external institutions to dominate our thoughts and to define who we are. This creates the space for the ego to play lots of control games in order to take what we need from each other.

Because this perspective sees our existence only from the point of view of the limitations of our physical existence, every person is potentially our competitor and every challenging experience we have becomes a matter of winning or losing. The most difficult people we meet are viewed as our greatest adversaries and the most demanding situations are perceived as potential failures. This way of thinking supports the idea that things happen *to* us and that our actions have no effect on what is happening. The assumption here is that *"they"* are hurting *"us,"* which leads to survival becoming the primary motivation for our existence.

When our perspective of life is that we have to compete with each other all the time, our energy feels contracted because we feel we have to constantly keep ourselves braced for the next attack. We tend to hold onto the anger, frustration, and pain involved with each negative experience and dwell on our mistakes instead of our life process of growth and learning.

Understandably, this point of view produces a great deal of stress because we feel we need to use all of our energy to protect our own interests.

The more we look to our outer world to provide us with our answers, the less centered we become. If we feel out of control of our own lives, we tend to want to dominate and control the actions of others in an effort to maintain some semblance of order.

If we see all of humanity as millions of independent entities who are disconnected from us, we are likely to behave as though our personal actions do not have any effect on others, and we can therefore justify hurting other people to get what we want for ourselves. This results in our playing endless versions of "energy tag," which have the underlying theme of "I've got what I want from you, now you go get what you need from someone else." When we do this, we are depleting someone else's energy for our regeneration rather than drawing on our limitless universal energy source.

Rather than perceiving life as a journey of spiritual growth and expansion, our life purpose becomes a quest for materialistic things such as power, control, fame, and money. Because material rewards only provide temporary satisfaction, we are likely to feel that we never have quite enough of anything, so we keep looking outside of ourselves to find fulfillment. We may get all the things we think we need in life, but something is still missing—our spirit feels squashed, and we feel empty inside.

At this point, we may have accomplished what we have set out to do, but we may not know who we have become in the process. When we lose sight of our identity and purpose, we have paid the ultimate price—we have lost our sense of true self.

This perspective of looking outside of ourselves for our answers produces a feeling that we are individually powerless to change things, so we find ourselves wanting to blame others for the situations in our lives. As we concentrate on all the external circumstances, we become self-hypnotized into believing that what we are seeing is the only possible reality, so we remain in this self-defeating loop by again looking to the outside to provide meaning in our lives.

The circle diagram on the following page illustrates the syndrome of living from the outside-in.

"LIVING FROM THE OUTSIDE-IN"
(Contraction of Energy)

Outer World - Source of authority is outside of self; Self-worth

defined by others

Body - Behavior is contrived to accommodate expectations of others

Mind - Perceptions based on the life theme that we need to use our energy to survive life

Spirit - Feeling of helplessness; Lack of self-identity

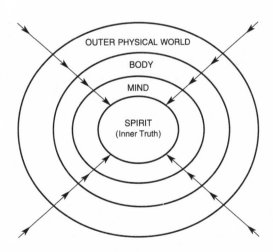

Why Does Living from
the Outside-In Contract Our Energy?

Perceiving our personal lives as being controlled by the outer world promotes a state of contraction that makes us feel like our world is coming in on us because we use our energy to react rather than create. We cope with the fear of losing our grip on life by holding on tighter—the more we wrestle with the resistance, the greater the resistance becomes. *Is it any wonder we feel depleted?* This stress can eventually lead to many physical ailments and diseases, one of which is depression. Is there anything more physically symbolic of sensing that our world is coming in on us than depression?

A former client of mine, Jason, was a classic example of a person whose life personified the model of living from the outside-in. I was inspired by Jason's courage in demonstrating that it is possible to change the direction of our lives at any time simply by choosing a different perspective. I share his true story in the hope that it will offer encouragement to the many people who suffer from depression.

When I met Jason, he was experiencing a life-threatening state of depression. The seeming catalyst for his depression was that he had just been laid off from his job. Money was no object for this gentleman, for he could have comfortably retired then and there. Or, if he chose to continue working, he had highly marketable skills for being hired by another firm.

From an external point of view, Jason had all the things in life which many consider to be ideal—he was well known in his profession, wealthy, married to a lovely woman, lived in a beautiful house in an upper-class neighborhood, and had healthy children. He kept agonizing over the same question:

"How," he kept asking himself, "could I possibly be so depressed? I have everything anyone could want."

Even with all of these blessings, as well as taking pre-scribed anti-depressant medication, his mental pain became so excruciating that he was dysfunctional and even suicidal.

Through our healing sessions, a loving family, and a couple of compassionate friends who had known their own dark nights of the soul, Jason was encouraged to make an honest assessment of his life by searching within his own spirit for his answers. His breakthrough came as soon as he became aware that he had based his self-worth completely on the outside-in perspective of what other people thought of him. He had equated his value as a person with what he did for a living and was rather surprised to realize that this was something he had done for most of his life. Jason realized that one of the reasons he was exhausted was that he was investing most of his energy focusing on the negatives in life. He also became aware that he had used his compulsive work habits to block out some painful relationships with people, many of whom he had not forgiven over the years. When he lost his job, he lost his pseudo self-identity, and the foundation of his outside-in existence crumbled. It is no wonder that he felt his life had ended.

Through the message of his pain, Jason awakened to the realization that he had not built his life on his inner truth. His recovery began immediately as he began to align his thoughts, words, and actions with a life theme of living from the inside-out. His life started to flow as he projected his genuine self, rather than the person he thought people wanted him to be. He shifted his focus from concentrating on all his problems to what he wanted to accomplish in life. Rather than ignore his emotions, as he had done so often in the past, Jason began to deal with his genuine feelings and to address his issues of forgiveness. He opened himself up to spiritual renewal by meditating, taking nature walks, reading inspirational books and poetry, and listening to classical music—activities he had previously viewed as unproductive. As he grew stronger, Jason developed a deep level of compassion and discovered that he also had the energy to reach out to help others as well.

He now gauges his success by the integrity with which he lives his life, not just by what he does for a living. Rather than perceiving the loss of his job as a personal failure, Jason shares with others that losing his job has been his most profound lesson and the greatest catalyst for turning his life around. Within a couple months of our first healing session, he became successfully self-employed, actively involved in many social causes, and is now truly enjoying a balanced life.

Jason's story is not unique. Though the loss of a job can be a major trigger in sparking an awareness that we are living from the outside-in, increasing numbers of us are being "brought to our knees" as our illusions of outer self-definition come crashing down.

Why Have So Many of Us Chosen This Perspective of Life?

We live in a society in which we are conditioned to focus primarily on outer stimulation. From earliest childhood, many of us were taught by well-intentioned parents and caretakers to define ourselves by what other people think of us. Seeking the approval of others quickly became the major motivation for most of our behavior patterns, starting very early in the lives of most of us. As a result, we developed a belief system that our self-worth is determined by the opinions of others rather than learning to develop our own sense of self-esteem based on inner values. Unless we became aware of this perception and chose to change it, we continued to perpetuate this belief into adulthood.

For example, most of us have been in numerous life situations where we have knocked ourselves out trying to please someone by being the selfless mother, wife, father, husband, child, sister, brother, friend, employer, or employee. We emotionally gave and gave until eventually we felt depleted. We were desperately seeking approval for our heroic deeds. When we did not get back what we considered an appropriate response, we felt totally unappreciated and, perhaps, even rejected. We were being "good," and yet we did not feel recognized and validated. We became angry and resentful, and round and round we went in an endless circle of desperately trying to get our own needs met because we have spent all of our energy taking care of everyone else.

When we give emotionally, mentally, and physically to others without honoring our own needs for spiritual nourishment, we are overlooking our own worthiness to receive. Predictably, we run out of energy. If we do not believe that we are connected to the non-material world of spirit, we have to look to someone else for our energy. Ironically, this seemingly selfless approach is far from selfless because it cultivates an environment where everyone is looking to everyone else to feel regenerated. Instead of giving of ourselves, we end up taking from others out of a desperate need to feel complete.

This is certainly no excuse to blame the people who raised us. They were doing the best they could with what they knew because it is what they also were taught as children. In fact, the sooner we stop blaming our parents and care givers for the way they raised us, the happier and more fulfilled we will be. We can spend our entire lives feeling out of control by holding others accountable for how we think, or we can create our own happiness by taking responsibility to expand our view of life to move closer to our spiritual truth.

How Do We Move Beyond the Perspective of Separation?

We can expand our outlook to a broader context of thinking by becoming aware of how the Perspective of Separation affects us on every level of our existence. When we perceive our mind, body, and inner spirit as separate from each other, we feel torn apart within our very own being because we are not honoring our whole self. Let's take a look at how this perspective affects each level of our existence, beginning with spirit.

How Does the Perspective of Separation Affect Our Inner Spirit?

The Perspective of Separation does not acknowledge the connection of our bodies and minds with spirit in this physical world. Some may believe that we will personally meet with the spiritual world only when we die or that there is no spiritual dimension of existence at all. Our physical self is the only aspect of ourselves we recognize. Though we certainly are physical beings, this perspective only validates our Earth Personality and ignores our infinitely larger Spiritual Self.

Seeing the spiritual plane of our existence as separate from our physical existence perpetuates a great deal of guilt and fear. This perspective causes many of us to cling to childhood concepts of an elusive Supreme Being with an overwhelming earth-like personality judging us from the spiritual dimension; such as, an authoritarian parent with a bad temper who punishes us when we have sinned, or a spiritual Santa Claus constantly watching over us taking notes of when we've been "good" or "bad," or perhaps a powerful celestial executive sitting behind a gigantic mahogany desk who grants and denies our requests depending on our performance.

Perceiving our spiritual source from a fearful perspective causes us to view life as a system of reward and punishment and implies that we are not innately good and worthy. **This lays the foundation for basing all our perceptions of life on lack of self-love.** If we feel this way about ourselves, then we believe this about other people and treat them accordingly. It's not hard to see that when the vast majority of our human population is clinging to the Perspective of Separation, we are, indeed, collectively creating a highly discordant world, within and outside ourselves.

How Does the Perspective of Separation Affect Our Bodies?

Separation is a context of thinking that views the body as a physical vehicle, independent of the mind and spirit. This is the modern scientific medical model prevalent in our Western Civilization which focuses attention and energy on the part or parts of the body which are in pain or are affected by disease without giving equal consideration to the mental and spiritual connections to the physical disorder.

If we treat the body separately from the mind, we are, in essence, saying that we do not believe our physical state of health is affected by our thoughts. Yet, in this day and age of high stress induced by competition and traumatic social and economic changes, can we honestly deny the tremendous impact that negative thoughts have in contributing to our physical problems? On the other side of the coin, there is an overwhelming amount of scientific evidence and personal testimonials which support the extraordinary power that positive thoughts have on our well-being, as is evident in mind-body healing processes such as prayer, psychotherapy, hypnosis, creative visualizations, relaxation meditations, bio-feedback, color therapy, music therapy, and a multitude of other natural healing techniques. The placebo effect, where the psychological impact of a sugar pill sometimes produces the same positive results as medication, is a wonderful example of the mind's ability to direct the body's recovery.

If we treat the body as detached from our inner spirit, we are not acknowledging the effect that our feelings have on our physical health. Most of us have experienced intensely challenging times of growth in our lives where our hearts have ached from enduring agonizing experiences, such as losing a loved one, serious illness, emotional or physical abuse, or divorce. Is it reasonable to believe that our bodies are not affected when we are feeling spiritually wounded? On the positive side, the reassuring voice of a kind physician, the touch of a loved one, the smile of approval from a parent, and a hug from a friend can go a long way in contributing to our physical health because the feelings of our soul are being honored.

How Does the Perspective of Separation Affect Our Minds?

If we view the mind as separate from body and spirit, we drastically reduce our brainpower. In essence, we limit the function of our brains by believing that we have to adopt an either/or method of thinking. In order to get a grasp on this insight, it is helpful to have a general understanding of the widely-accepted scientific concept supporting the theory that we all have two hemispheres within our brains. Many of us are already familiar with the terms, "right-brain" and "left-brain" thinking. Although we use both hemispheres of our brain in most of our activities, each hemisphere processes information differently.

The following two paragraphs summarize some of the functions of the left and right hemispheres of our brain, as discussed in the book, *The Right-Brain Experience*, by Marilee Zdenek:

The **Left Hemisphere**, also known as the left-brain, is the logical hemisphere and controls the right side of the body. It is associated with self-survival skills such as:

Linear Thinking – **Seeing the parts rather than the whole;** processing information sequentially
Analyzing – Evaluating factual material; logical reasoning
Verbal – Reading, talking, and writing
Literal – Interpreting words
Mathematical – Understanding numbers and symbols

Eastern Civilization calls this part of our being *Yang*, or the masculine part of the energy within each of us, which interprets and acts upon information. The left-brain is guided by the logical thought processes of our minds. We typically associate the left hemisphere with the aggressive side of our behavior, which emphasizes strength and the qualities of self.

The *Right Hemisphere*, also known as the right-brain, is the intuitive hemisphere and controls the left side of the body. It is associated with our creative skills, such as:

Non-Linear Thinking – **Seeing things as a whole;** processing many types of information simultaneously; flashes of insight
Non-Verbal – Receiving information through images and intuitive sensing
Spatial – Ability to identify location within space, such as putting together a puzzle or having a sense of direction within a new area
Imaginative – Seeing visions, dreaming, and fantasizing
Metaphoric – Perceiving through allegories and figures

of speech rather than literal interpretation

Artistic and Musical – Drawing, painting, and innate
   musical talent

Emotional – Being in touch with our feelings

Spiritual – Expressing the inner spirit; meditation; prayer

Eastern Civilization calls this part of our being *Yin*, or the feminine part of the energy within all of us. It is the right part of our brain which can directly tap into the unlimited field of universal intelligence. Information which comes through the right-brain is unmodified by the interpretation of the logic of our left-brain. The right-brain is guided by our spirit and is made evident to us through intuitive feelings of the heart. We typically associate the right hemisphere with the passive side of our behavior which emphasizes gentleness and an awareness of the qualities of others.

While it is true that our genes and chromosomes determine our gender, every person has the capacity to express both feminine (Yin) and masculine (Yang) energy.

Even though most of us favor one hemisphere more than the other in the way we process information, the truth is that each of us has the ability to utilize both hemispheres of our brains. However, if we concede to the Perspective of Separation, we are likely to subconsciously polarize our thinking by stereotyping ourselves as either a "left-brain personality" or a "right-brain personality"—as though we have to function exclusively as one or the other. In effect, we split our minds into an internal mental battle of the logic of the left-brain (guided by the ego) versus the intuition of the right-brain (guided by the spirit).

The reality is that the two hemispheres of our brain are partners on the same team! When we delude ourselves into thinking that we cannot concurrently assimilate the holistic insights of our right-brain with the discerning nature of our left-brain, we greatly underestimate our amazing human capabilities to do both. For example, an author draws upon the right hemisphere for the inspiration, feelings, and holistic concepts that are necessary to write a book, but the left hemisphere translates the insights and emotions into words. A scientist utilizes his well-educated left-brain for logic and analysis; however, it is the intuition of his right hemisphere that frequently allows his mind to leap to major insights which transcend previous theories and paradigms.

Albert Einstein is a wonderful example of a highly evolved person who actively expressed both types of hemispheric thinking. Although he was deeply entrenched in the analytical world of quantum physics, he implicitly trusted his intuition. He openly expressed his desire to ride on a light beam and told people that he thought in images and symbols rather than words. This type of integrated thinking allowed him to go way beyond where anyone else had dared to dream at that point in time.

When we stereotype ourselves as either a left-brain personality or a right-brain personality, we inhibit our natural human potential to integrate the wisdom of our non-material world of spirit into the knowledge of our material world.

The "Left-Brain Personality" Stereotype

Due to the fact that our society stresses survival and competition, most of us emphasize the use of our left-brain. Because our left-brain perceives the parts, rather than the whole, we are likely to acknowledge only logical thinking as being valid. If we brand our-selves as a left-brain thinker (and the majority of the population does), we are likely to confine our thinking with the paradigm that no idea or concept can possibly be acceptable or believable unless proven by concrete, deductive reasoning. Limiting our attitude to this way of thinking restricts our informational input to the linear screening processes of the left-brain.

This automatically blocks the much broader wisdom and larger possibilities being presented by the right-brain. Instead of seeing the mind as the connecting channel between the spiritual and physical realms, our human ego places the mind over the spirit as the ultimate authority. We then judge other people's ideas as right or wrong, depending on whether they share in our particular hemispheric approach to thinking.

I know of two brothers, Paul and Jerry, who love each other dearly and yet, because Paul has confined his view of life to provable concepts, it is getting increasingly difficult for them to communicate. Paul, a talented computer specialist, is extremely knowledgeable about technology. Because the nature of his work focuses on the technical world of concrete thinking, he is in the habit of viewing not only his work from this analytical aspect, but also his entire world. He has adopted the "If you can't prove it to me, it can't be true" attitude. His brother, Jerry, an entrepreneur and visionary, focuses more on the big picture of life and is very open to investigating the non-conventional insights of the spiritual dimension. Jerry finds it very difficult to discuss his feelings and ideas with his brother because Paul usually immediately rebuffs anything that cannot be explained by logic. Because Jerry feels rejected and unheard when he tries to talk with his brother, he doesn't discuss things with him too often anymore. Unfortunately Paul is not receiving the benefit of the richness of his brother's vast insights, nor the broadening of his own perceptions, because he has closed off his right-brain input.

Ideas, by their very nature, are inspired by our spirit and become evident to us through the function of the right hemisphere. If we are not open to receiving the intuitive insights and messages which come to us spontaneously, we are splitting our spiritual self from our physical self.

The intuitive right-brain says, "This is truth," and our rational left-brain says, " I don't understand, therefore it cannot be."

If we opt to believe in and act upon only the concrete logic of the left hemisphere, eventually we will not trust in our innate ability to receive the phenomenal insights of universal wisdom which are gifted to us in the form of instant insights, dreams, flashes of imagination, and gut level feelings.

Sadly, this left-brain-only perspective divides us within our very own minds and separates us from those who perceive the larger picture of life, as well as from our own ability to do so. It is rooted in fear of the unknown and blocks us from the infinite possibilities of the spirit in favor of the finite knowledge of the mind.

The "Right-Brain Personality" Stereotype

If we label ourselves as "right-brain thinkers," we may become so preoccupied with receiving the intuitive messages of the spirit that we have difficulty translating our ideas into physical action. Although we are receptive to seeing the whole of a picture or idea, our Perspective of Separation generates a fear of not knowing how to incorporate our intuitive messages into our lives.

We might receive an intuitive flash or gut-level feeling that we need to write a book, become an entrepreneur, immediately telephone a friend, or spontaneously take a trip, but do nothing about it. When we have intuitive insights but we don't act upon them, we are also separating our spiritual self from our physical self. This results in the paradoxical feelings of, "I totally believe in the truth of my spirit, but I do not believe in my personal ability to act upon it." While it is of paramount importance that we be open to receiving the spiritual messages of the right-brain, it is equally essential that we put them into action through the capabilities of the left-brain. My friend, Sally, personifies this type of internal struggle:

Sally is a corporate consultant with many years of experience. Sally is very in touch with her feelings and the feelings of others and is completely open to listening to her intuition. For five years she has had an intense desire to leave her traditional job and become an author. Her spirit speaks to her constantly through dreams, friends, flashes of imagination, and a relentless underlying passion to express her deepest truth through writing. She continues to hold back from making the transition because she is afraid to trust her ability to bring her ideas into actual action. Even though she continues to rationalize the impracticality of making a career switch, her inner truth tenaciously continues to speak to her of a deeper life purpose, and each day she feels more inner conflict. Sally is waiting for a cosmic kick to make her leave her job. The truth is that she is already getting one! The indications are everywhere—she is just afraid to acknowledge them.

This way of thinking is also rooted in the fear-based Perspective of Separation and blocks us from honoring the divine gift we humans have been given to bring the wisdom of the spirit into tangible, physical form.

Our whole self is capable of balanced thinking which integrates the function of both the left and right hemispheres of the brain. As we create unity and balance within our individual minds, we integrate and balance our "world brain" as well.

What Is Meant by Our "World Brain?"

Just as each person has a left and right-brain function, so does our world mind, which is the collective thoughts of all of us who live on earth. Historically, we have individually, and as a world society, concentrated on developing the left-brain function. The left-brain of our world can be compared to the predominant influence of technology in our society and the overall bottom line mentality of business. This is the masculine (yang) energy within us which emphasizes power, aggression, and awareness of self.

For centuries we have diligently explored the body and mind aspects of our human nature and our relationship to our environment through the wonders of science and technology, which have produced astounding accomplishments: we can travel to the moon and back, hop a jet in New York and be in London in less than four hours, save lives by transplanting the internal organs of one person into another, see and hear each other from all corners of the world twenty-four hours a day through the media of television, radio, and telephone, and instantly communicate with almost anyone anywhere in the world about any topic at any time through computer technology. The more we learn about ourselves and our universe, the closer we move toward comprehending the whole of our human existence.

While left-brain, aggressive energy is an absolutely essential part of our human growth, our human species is becoming imbued with too much of it. The overwhelming greed, crime, and violence we are presently experiencing are indications that our collective masculine energy has tipped out of balance. We have acquired tremendous knowledge and information; but information is power, and power is dangerous if it is not balanced with benevolent conscience.

The spiritual aspect of our global mentality can be compared to the right-brain, feminine (yin) energy within all of us which focuses on intuitive feelings, gentleness, and the good of the whole. The inner and outer turmoil which we are experiencing is the energy of our spiritual consciousness innately guiding us to be moral and to use our energy for the well-being of the universe.

We are now moving into a stage of our evolution where it is in our greatest good to integrate the exciting theoretical concepts of our technological, material world with the dynamic and boundless possibilities which exist in our intuitive, non-material world, beginning at the level of self. In fact, we are seeing encouraging signs all around us indicating that we have already begun the process of integrating our personal spiritual values into our societal institutions as we move toward the more enlightened Perspective of Oneness.

How Can We Possibly Interpret the Turmoil We Are Experiencing As a Sign That Our Society Is Moving Toward the Perspective of Oneness?

Our society is the outward manifestation of the inner values of all of us. Although painful and, on an exterior level, chaotic, the changes we are seeing are dramatic indications that our personal conscience is kicking in. We are no longer functioning as a society thinking *en masse* and buying into the myth that our personal lives are changed by our outer social institutions. **Most of the social changes which are happening are bubbling up from the individual level, indicating we are awakening, one by one, to the awareness that our outer world can be healed only through the paths of our personal lives.** We can see encouraging evidence of this personal consciousness by taking an overview of the conditions within some of our major social structures:

Our Business Structure

Many companies have undergone enormous reorganization processes and are experiencing major employee morale problems, particularly over the last decade. The hierarchical management concept still prevalent today was conceived during the Industrial Revolution as a way to teach the ways of the business world to people migrating into the cities from rural farming communities. It is a system of management based on control and dominion, and one which makes a distinct separation between management and the employee body of an organization. What was once an effective way to run companies has become outdated because today's employees are much more sophisticated and knowledgeable about their jobs. In addition, the complexity of business brought on by technological advances and world-wide competition makes it impossible for a few people at the top to contain most of the intelligence of an organization.

At the outset, it appeared that the only group to benefit from reorganizations and layoffs was senior management and ownership because they were able to immediately cut back expenses; however, a boomerang effect is manifesting—many people who otherwise might never have ventured out on their own have discovered the joys and rewards of self-employment or have changed careers completely. Increasing numbers of displaced employees, who at first felt they had lost the source of their identity when they lost their jobs, have redefined their life priorities by putting family values and personal ethics at the top of the list. More and more employees are now unwilling to make major personal sacrifices which allow their work to detract from the quality of their family and personal lives, such as excessive work hours and frequent transfers. As employees, we are awakening to our true inner callings for more meaningful and flexible work. We are also realizing that we cannot delegate responsibility for the security and quality of our personal lives to our employers.

The values of management are also shifting to a more spiritual focus. As employers, we are realizing that employees do not park their spiritual values at home while taking their minds and bodies to work. An article in *Fortune Magazine*, "Why Do We Work?" states that when scores of managers were asked why they worked, "the three most common reasons cited, besides paying the mortgage, were to make the world a better place, to help themselves and others on their team grow spiritually and intellectually, and to perfect their technical skills."

Companies are increasingly responding to the need for employees to have a balanced work/personal life by offering benefits such as: in-home offices, telecommuting, job sharing, flex time, onsite physical fitness facilities, meditation rooms, onsite child care, and both maternity and paternity leaves of absence.

The impetus for these changes is being initiated from the bottom up, contrary to our former paradigm of thinking that major corporate changes have to come from the top down. The role of business management is in the process of transitioning from being a boss who has control over employees to that of a leader whose mission is to guide, inspire, and facilitate the collective intelligence of an organization.

A business organization is not a structure with a life of its own; it is the living, breathing collective consciousness of all the people who are a part of it. As employers and employees unify in their visions to make the workplace a process of human growth and development, the social purpose of the entire organization evolves to a higher objective—service to humanity. As this happens, increased profits become the result of a balanced, internally motivated workforce with a common purpose rather than the start point from which all decisions are made.

The new organizations and reorganizations we are seeing are evidence that the corporate world is beginning to reflect a major shift in our personal consciousness as we integrate profit-making with the betterment of our planet.

Our Health Care System

Medical technology has unveiled brilliant discoveries which can save our lives and prolong our life expectancy through its ever-increasing knowledge and insights about the functions of the human mind and body. The pharmaceutical drugs and surgical procedures which have resulted from modern scientific studies are amazingly effective in dealing with trauma and curing serious illnesses; however, we have become so enamored with and dependent upon scientific technology and the study of pathology and drugs, that we have lost sight of the human spirit and the body's magnificent ability to heal itself.

There is a difference between curing and healing. Curing works from the outside-in beginning with the symptoms of the physical malady; and healing works from the inside-out, beginning with the reason for the pain or illness. We can sometimes cure our symptoms externally; but true healing works at all levels of our human existence—mind, body, and spirit.

It is self-defeating to divide ourselves into the right/wrong posture of the Western Civilization concept of medicine versus the Eastern Civilization concept of natural healing—both avenues are seated in an intention to help people get well. We have evolved to a time in our human evolution when we are being called upon to integrate our technical knowledge with the wisdom of our innate natural healing power by treating the whole person (mind, body and spirit), not just the body.

We are beginning to shift our focus from illness to wellness. Natural healing techniques, once viewed as non-traditional "alternative" medicine, are beginning to be termed as "complementary" medicine as the main-stream medical community accepts holistic healing concepts.

We are witnessing a major cultural change in medicine as the paths of traditional and alternative medicine converge and become *integrative medicine*. Contrary to the past when medical trends were dictated by physicians, this shift is being initiated at the consumer level as individuals educate themselves in the vast array of natural alternatives to allopathic medicine and demand that doctors offer choices of health care treatments. This is largely due to the fact that we are

awakening to our personal responsibility to actively participate in the healing of our own bodies.

Our Academic System

We have graduated from the one-room school houses of
colonial times, where a student was taught a few subjects by
the same teacher for several years, to the highly specialized
departmental schools of today in which we offer advanced
levels of every imaginable subject taught by numerous teachers with impressive academic credentials.

The educational industry's purpose is to prepare our children to use their knowledge to understand their mission in life
and to experience it in all its aspects. Yet, in many ways, our
educational system has become the same hierarchical structure as business. Teachers have gotten caught in a role of
responding to layer-upon-layer of a bureaucracy urging
them to produce smarter children, not wiser children. Our
educational system has measured the academic success of
our children by achievement tests based on rote learning
rather than emphasizing the applied knowledge and wisdom
so necessary for them to fashion a life on this earth. We have
equated test scores with intelligence and have leaned toward
catering to the students with the highest scores, while those
with average and below average scores are many times merely
tolerated and allowed to pass through.

Parents and educators are breaking away from the structures of our current educational system by coming together
to focus on a more holistic concept of education: *life-long
learning*. We are realizing that if our schools are to deliver a
forum for the expression and application of our children's
spiritual wisdom, then our teachers need to become facilita-
tors of learning rather than teachers of knowledge. Honoring
the spirit of our children by encouraging them to express
their own visions of what they want to accomplish with their
lives and designing curriculums that nurture and support
their individual aspirations are primary considerations in the
self-directed learning programs which are rapidly beginning

to surface in our school systems. Guided by parents, teachers, and school administrators, students design curriculums that nurture and support their individual aspirations while still meeting academic requirements.

The dramatic increase in students being diagnosed as having "learning differences" is a powerful spiritual message to our society that we need to honor the unique learning styles of individuals by developing learning models that are not only theoretical, but experiential as well. We are just beginning to see a student's overall capabilities in more holistic terms than just pure left-brained academics, thereby acknowledging the right-brain's capacity for creativity, imagination, and vision of the whole. Furthermore, recognizing the benefits of developing well-rounded, civic-minded citizens, many schools are developing the life skills of students and preparing them for community service by including group and individual community programs in their curriculum requirements. For example, the entire Chicago public school system has implemented a community service requirement for all high school students.

Educating the whole child, respecting the uniqueness of each student, and perceiving learning as a life-long process are positive indications of a society moving toward teaching its children how to live from the integrity of spirit.

Our Political System

Our government was formed to provide a common defense and to promote the general welfare of its constituents. We have been successful in creating an effective national defense; however, our governmental system has evolved into an unwieldy organization serving the interests of too few of its citizens.

Our political system focuses on two major objectives: First, to get the office holder re-elected or re-appointed; and secondly, to use the power of the office to serve the greatest good of the office holder's political party. In order to be elected, each candidate has to acquire funds to launch and maintain a successful campaign. Donations, the main source of funds, create a difficult set of problems for the candidate. The *quid-pro-quo* attached to larger donations sometimes causes a politician to stray from serving the greatest good of all by backing the particular needs of major donors. In order to avoid being beholden to any special interest group, a politician must spend his/her own money for a campaign. This begets a political system that is either indebted to the contributors or is composed of mostly the wealthy. In either case, the greatest good of all cannot be served.

The answer to this dilemma is rapidly advancing on the world scene. Technology may soon replace the existing representative forms of governments with a truly democratic form of government in which everyone can vote on every issue, and political leaders are freed to truly serve all the people. This trend has already begun as shown by the explosion of ballot initiatives offered on election days in which voters have a direct vote on a particular issue. Moreover, as the two large parties of the country alienate an increasing number of voters, the number of alternate parties, as well as the membership within them, continues to rise, such as the Reform Party, Libertarians, the Greens, and the Natural Law Party.

We are also seeing the breakdown of traditional country boundaries in economic activities. The twentieth century has seen a dramatic lowering of trade obstacles and tariffs and an explosion in international trade, intimately linking the economies of the world. The global financial challenges illustrate the high degree of interdependence between the world's countries. The European Economic Union and the Euro Dollar, ultimate examples of this kind of interdependence, are harbingers of a single economic world structure. This global economic interconnection may well lead to a kind of world government elected by everyone, serving the greatest good of the entire planet and dedicated to peace and prosperity of all.

Our Religious System

For thousands of years people have looked to religion as

a source of spiritual guidance, strength, support, comfort, and a sense of community. Most religions originally emerged from our collective human perception sensing there is a creative Supreme Being beyond our physical world which supports all of life. Although each religion pursues a different path, most major religions seek to reconnect with divine love and to obey the principles of spiritual truth.

However, as time has evolved, many of our religious organizations have departed from the true meaning of religion and obedience. The root word of religion is *religare*, meaning to *reconnect*, and to *bind back*, and the root word of obey is *obodio*, meaning to *listen*. In its purest sense, religion is the process of *reconnecting* with divine love by *listening* to our inner voice. Our collective perception of religion has moved toward external ritual rather than an internal process of perpetual spiritual growth. Many of us have forgotten that our specific religions are the paths which guide us to the greater truth of our unity with our spiritual source, not the ultimate truth within itself. All too often we have used our religions to distinguish our differences rather than to draw us together.

Many religious perceptions are rooted in the fear created by our human ego rather than the unconditional love of spirit. For example, when our religions teach the concept of a Supreme Being which is separate from our physical existence, is this promoting a perspective which acknowledges our spiritual connection and divinity within, or is this a Perspective of Separation which encourages us to look outside of ourselves for spiritual renewal and self-validation? When our religions teach us the concept of a Supreme Being judging us from afar and deeming us to be innately sinful, is this encouraging self-love or self-deprecation? The message "this is the only path" implies that there is one religion which has found the only way to human salvation to the exclusion of all others. Is this love or is this self-righteous judgment? If a religious cult is centered around worshiping and fearfully following the instructions of its human leader, is this divine love or is this human ego? When we fight "religious wars," is this love or is this hate?

These are questions which we can only answer for our-

selves. However, many people are actively and openly
beginning to question whether the doctrines and beliefs of
the religions to which they belong are in alignment with their
inner values, or whether they want to belong to any religion
at all. We are awakening to the true meaning of religion and
a sense of our direct spiritual connection with divine love.

Increasingly, people are realizing we each have the power
to look within our inner spirit to find truth and life purpose.
There has been a major shift over the past thirty years in
which people are leaving the more mainstream, doctrinally
and intellectually centered religious denominations to those
focused more on personal spiritual connection and Oneness
with Spirit, such as Pentecostal and "New Age" groups.
Whether we decide to be a part of a religion or not, many people are beginning to take responsibility to live their lives from
the core of their personal integrity and spiritual values.

Religions are increasingly responding to this individual
awareness by shifting their focus from outward social issues
and dogma to focusing on inner spiritual life. George Barna in
his book, *The Leading Spiritual Indicators*, says that
"America is transitioning from a Christian nation to a spiritually diverse society. This results in a new perception of religion: a personalized, customized form of faith views which
meet personal needs, minimize rules and absolutes, and bear
little resemblance to the 'pure' form of any of the world's
major religions."

Rather than focusing on whose way is the right way, our
religions are beginning to merge into one path moving toward
a common vision of unity and oneness.

Chapter Four

The Perspective of Oneness

As humanity matures and our spiritual awareness increases, we are growing beyond the Perspective of Separation because we are realizing that living from the outside-in does not reflect the truth of our whole self. Individually and collectively we are moving toward the much broader world view of seeing life from the spiritual Perspective of Oneness.

The Perspective of Oneness is a holistic view of life which embraces the interconnection of our individual minds and bodies with our inner spirit; our spiritual connection with each other; and our human connection with the universe. From this point of view, we see our existence in the material world and non-material world as a simultaneous experience, and we acknowledge that our whole self is both matter and energy.

When we see life from the Perspective of Oneness, we live from the inside-out by basing the theme of our life purpose on our inner spiritual values rather than our human ego, which seeks approval from our outer, material world. This is a model of living whereby we derive our energy from our universal source rather than taking it from others; and we base our lives on the unconditional love of spirit rather than the fear of surviving our outer world. It is a perspective of life which perpetuates an environment of kindness, respect, and cooperation because it is rooted in our inner spiritual truth.

How Do We Know What
Our Inner Spiritual Truth Is?

There is a Hindu legend which says that at one point in time humanity had abused its divine powers so greatly that the gods convened to discuss what to do about it. They decided the best course of action was to remove it and hide it—but where? After careful consideration they unanimously decided there was one place where divine power could be hidden where humans would never even think to look—deep within ourselves.

Our divine power is our inner spiritual truth. For ages we have looked outside of ourselves to find it when, indeed, we have always had it inside of our hearts. Spiritual truth is not something we need to be taught—it is the memory of who we truly are and why we are here. We access our truth through our intuition. Intuition is our communications link to the universal field of energy. It is the inner voice constantly whispering messages to us of things which are for the good of our personal spiritual growth. Because we are all of one spirit, what is in our personal greatest good is also in the best interests of all of us.

Intuition is our innate human power to instantaneously access information from the field of universal intelligence without conscious reasoning. In essence, we are each a conduit for a constant stream of limitless wisdom. Because intuition is a right-brain function, it isn't something we can analyze with our minds; rather, it is something we feel at a gut level. We sometimes refer to these feelings as sixth sense, inner wisdom, inner knowing, and flashes of imagination. Many of us actually experience physical sensations when we hear or see something which coincides with our truth. We may suddenly get goose bumps, feel a tingling sensation, spontaneously take a deep breath, feel an electrical current going up our backs, or sense an overall wave of energy. These sensations are indications that our minds and bodies are literally resonating with the energetic frequency of the truth of spirit. We can also get physical indications when something we are hearing or seeing is not truth. Usually it is a contracted feeling, such as a knot in the stomach or throat, shortness of breath, or a sudden chill.

Although we all sense it in different ways, and some of us even deny sensing it at all, *every* person has intuition—it is part of our human nature. The reason it appears that not all of us have intuition is simply because some of us listen to and act upon our inner messages, whereas others simply dismiss them as insignificant. We many times ignore our intuition because we want to validate our intuitive messages with our left-brain logic and analysis. When we attempt to do this, we choke the flow of intuitive information coming through to us because messages of the spirit are infinitely larger than the logical paradigms of our mind.

We can also distinguish *intuitive* messages from *impulsive* messages. When we get an *impulsive* message, it is usually initiated by our ego in the form of a whim to immediately do something whether it is good for us or not. Our impulse may be to indulge in an addictive behavior, such as overeating, or to run out and buy the first car we see. If it is an impulse, chances are we will change our minds if we wait for a while or sleep on the idea. Also, we often feel guilty or unfulfilled after acting impulsively. *Intuitive* messages, on the other hand, are relentless and persistent. Even when we ignore them, they have the tenacious habit of resurfacing time and time again. If, for example, buying the first car we see is an intuitive message, we will feel even more strongly about the idea after we have slept on it. If buying the car is an intuitive message, the universe will also open up the possibilities to make it happen. While impulsive messages may or may not be in our greatest good, intuitive messages are always in our best interests, causing us to feel uplifted and fulfilled.

Although our intuitive connection is available to us twenty-four hours a day, seven days a week, we are sometimes so frenzied by outside stimulation that we have to create a personal space of silence in order to move into a receptive frame of mind that enables us to listen. This can be done through prayer and numerous types of meditation, or by doing things that are as simple as taking a deep breath, sitting still while concentrating on our breathing, taking a walk, listening to soft music, or taking a soothing, warm bath. We can use any technique we choose—the important thing is that we find a way to center ourselves in peace and balance our energy.

Because intuition connects us with our Oneness of spirit, the messages it reveals to us are always rooted in unconditional love and pure truth. We develop a sensitivity to perceiving these internal messages by listening, trusting, and acting upon them. The more we do this, the more we empower ourselves to live our lives from the inside-out.

What Does Living from the "Inside-Out" Mean?

Living from the inside-out is a model of life which evolves from viewing the world from the Perspective of Oneness and is based on spiritual values and cooperating for the good of the whole. When we see the world from this vantage point, our lives become an expanded, visible expression of our inner spirit. The center of our existence is our very soul, and it is the highest authority for everything we do. Accordingly, we hold ourselves accountable to think and act in a way that conforms with our own internal standards of integrity.

Our self-worth is determined by how we feel about ourselves rather than how we want other people to perceive us. We access our inner truth by listening to our intuitive inner wisdom and acting in accordance with our gut-level feelings of what is correct.

We honor our individual uniqueness, which results in thoughts and actions that reflect who we genuinely are. Because we are projecting our authentic self, we attract people and circumstances which support our well-being, and we find we are supported with what we need when we need it.

When we perceive life as a dynamic process of spiritual growth, everyone is our teacher and every experience is an opportunity to become more of who we truly are. We embrace the truth that many times our most meaningful experiences come from the people whom we see as most difficult and the situations which are most challenging. When we see life as an adventure, each experience is an opportunity to evolve to greater levels of insight and wisdom. Because there is no winning or losing, only different ways to learn and grow, we are inspired to cooperate with others in working together for the good of the whole.

Rather than a quest for material things, we see that our life purpose is to remember how to love ourselves and others by aligning our perceptions and actions with our inner truth. When our personal integrity serves as the center for our lives, we use our energy to create what we want rather than to survive. We see life as a reflection of ourselves and take responsibility for the role we have played in creating the world, and we realize that we also have the power to play a role in changing it for the better.

As we reclaim our inner power, we become energized because we see ourselves at the center of our existence rather than a victim of it. As our energy increases, we are better able to nurture ourselves mentally, emotionally, physically, and spiritually, which encourages total health. This puts us in a situation where we have the endurance and motivation to assist others to help themselves.

This point of view encourages a state of expansion because we are contributing the gift of ourselves to the world. We feel inspired to be compassionate with others because there is a level of excitement in sharing with others when we are living a life based on our own inner convictions. When we center our lives around our spiritual core, we are living in harmony with the Oneness of spirit, creating unity and harmony within our inner personal lives and our outer world.

The illustration below demonstrates living our lives from the inside-out.

"LIVING FROM THE INSIDE-OUT "
(Expansion of Energy)

Spirit -   Source of authority is inner truth; Self-worth is based on spiritual values

Mind -   Thoughts are based on perceptions that we use our energy to create our reality

Body -   Behavior coincides with personal inner values

Outer World -   Reflection of real self; Confirmation of self-worth; Experiences coincide with inner truth; **Opens us to limitless potential**

LIMITLESS POSSIBILITIES

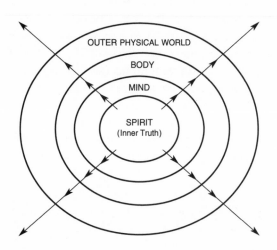

What Is Oneness of Spirit?

Regardless of our race, nationality, sex, creed, age, or socioeconomic status, we are one human family interdependent and interconnected with each other and with all the elements of nature. Although we are each different in appearance and expression, we walk the earth together and share the same sun, moon, stars, oceans, and sky with each other, as well as with the animals, flowers, trees, grass, and rocks. The way we take care of our planet is the way it takes care of us. When any part of our ecosystem is out of balance, we become individually and collectively imbalanced. When an animal, plant, or mineral becomes depleted, we lose a part of ourselves. Like a circle of dominoes, what affects any one of us automatically impacts every one of us.

As mentioned in Chapter One, our minds and bodies, as well as all living matter, are sustained by a common life force, or universal field. This life force of energy is referenced by many other names, some of which are: God, Spiritual Consciousness, Collective Consciousness, Infinite Intelligence, Infinite Potential, Universal Intelligence, The Universe, Cosmic Consciousness, Nature's Intelligence, and the Field of All Possibilities. Whatever name we choose, it includes the collective spiritual essence of every soul within existence. Each one of us is part of this unified spiritual bond of Oneness, and it is a part of us. Just as we cannot divide our individual minds and bodies from our spirit, we cannot separate the spiritual union we have with each other and all of creation. The root word of Spirit means *breath*. We are sharing one universe with every breath we take! Believing that we need to wait until we die to meet our spiritual self is like holding our breath until we find air. Our spirit is the breath of air that is right here, right now in this wondrous world of physical matter. We can no more separate ourselves from spirit than we can isolate the air from our lungs.

Whatever differences we may have in our personal and religious perceptions, studies consistently show that the majority of our world population believes in a spiritual Supreme Being. In fact, a recent Gallup Poll states: "92% of Americans believe in God." There is also a widespread belief in the process of atonement, which is our human unification with this Supreme Being. Breaking the word atonement into three parts, AT-ONE-MENT, is an extremely significant indication of an almost universal awareness of the Oneness of our human spirit. The terms we use to describe the ultimate source of our existence are very personal and depend upon our individual beliefs; however, it is profoundly apparent that there are certain common denominators in our perceptions. One is that most of us believe this Supreme Being is a being of perfect love, and another is that most of the different names which have consistently been used by the vast majority of religions, cultures, and individuals since recorded history to describe a Supreme Spiritual Being have the common sound of *aah*; i.e. *God, Adonoi, Yahweh, Allah,* and *Jehovah. Aah* is the sound of creation and the spontaneous sound we make when we take in a breath.

When we view life from the Perspective of Oneness, we do not perceive the source of creation as a spiritual authoritarian personality outside of us who exerts power and judgment over humanity, nor as a concrete religious concept which can be proven by the logical mentality of our physical world. Perhaps many of the people who say they do not believe in a Supreme Being are not so much denying the existence of a higher spiritual reality as they are objecting to confining its infinite potential within the context of a human-like personality. From the Perspective of Oneness, our source of creation defies definition because it is more powerful than our physical selves and surpasses the barriers of any of our human words, thoughts, and concepts. It is so immense and profound that trying to confine it to finite human perception is like trying to imprison all light. Although the nature of our human mind longs for an answer, it is more of an eternal question deep within our soul perpetually and instinctively inspiring us to reach toward greater love, truth, and wholeness.

Since we cannot define our Supreme Being in human concepts, we can only *experience* it as a constantly emerging process of spiritual unfoldment and the boundless, loving energy of life within and all around us. We can feel it in our hearts as unity, expansion, and wholeness. To feel Oneness is to awaken to a deep memory within our spirit recalling a personal connection to light and universal love. Oneness can be sensed by our hearts as the bond of unconditional love that unifies all of creation.

Is Spirituality the Same Thing As Religion?

The terms *spirituality* and *religion* are frequently used interchangeably; however, they do not mean the same thing.

A religion is a social structure, created by humans, based on a system of beliefs, attitudes, and practices. There are many different religions in the world. Most of them have chosen a particular path to follow in our eternal human quest for deeper truth and love. We may choose to belong to a particular religion due to family tradition, life experiences, a desire to be with people of like mind, and many other personal reasons. We can also choose not to belong to any religion at all.

Spirit, the breath of life, is an innate part of who we are. Whether we belong to a religion or not, every human being has a spirit because we are all part of creation. We do not need to choose it, nor do we need to do anything to be chosen. Like breath, it simply is. We each have a direct spiritual connection with the unconditional love of a higher reality, and we are each free to choose how we want to perceive it. There is nothing we need to do to qualify in order to be worthy of making this direct connection and it is not necessary to have an intermediary to access it.

What Is Unconditional Love?

Unconditional love is not something that happens to us or outside of us. It is the life force of energy *within* our very being and is ingrained in every cell of our bodies. We don't have to search for love—we *are*, each one of us, the physical embodiment of unconditional love! When we remember that we are created in love, our earthly perceptions of seeing man as an inconsequential speck within the universe give way to the infinite spiritual truth—we are, each one of us, the ultimate expression of creation!

Because unconditional love is life energy, it is formless, infinite, constantly in motion, and limitless in its potential. Universal love is neutral, all forgiving, and knows no judgment. It is available to everyone without discernment, and there is absolutely nothing we need to do to qualify for it.

Unconditional love has a positive effect on both the biological physical plane and the spiritual metaphysical plane, creating truth, joy, beauty, health, harmony, and everything in the world that is in our greatest good. The benevolent, compassionate nature of universal love flows through us and blesses everyone and everything it touches.

When we open our hearts to receiving and expressing the love of the universe, we feel expansive and radiant. We automatically rise above the limitations of fear because love is infinitely more powerful than fear; in fact, unconditional love is the most powerful force in existence. There is no amount of darkness that can blot out light; yet the tiniest amount of light can overcome darkness. This means that no matter how dark and chaotic our lives may seem at times, we can find comfort in knowing that our earthly world is always held within an infinitely larger context of universal love and light.

Universal love is the energy of healing and is at a frequency that is so high it defies our human comprehension. The higher the frequency, the greater the capability for healing and harmonizing. When we focus our thoughts on unconditional love, our personal vibration escalates, enabling us to receive the healing energies of the universe mentally, emotionally, physically, and spiritually. When we are individually functioning at a high frequency, we resonate and attract other people and situations also working in accordance with the energy of love because our thoughts are magnetic. By doing this, we create a personal reality in which we are constantly nourished and supported by the healing energies of each other. As humanity becomes more aware of its spirituality, our collective vibration continues to escalate, enabling us to heal faster and faster. Perhaps this explains why more and more people are responding to vibrational forms of healing, such as acupuncture, magnetic therapy, homeopathy, and herbal medicine.

When we make a conscious decision to choose thoughts based on unconditional love, we commit ourselves to expressing respect, kindness, and honesty to ourselves and in all our relationships. The more we incorporate these qualities into our behavior, the more sacred our lives become.

What Is a Sacred Life?

Many of us feel that our lives are an elusive struggle to find our spiritual purpose. Usually when we feel this way, we are looking for an answer outside of ourselves, like the perfect job to come along, winning the lottery, or finding the perfect mate. We may also think we have to withdraw from ordinary life and retreat to a spiritual or religious sanctuary in order to discover our life purpose.

This proves to be very frustrating because our life purpose cannot be defined by outside labels and circumstances, nor do we need to separate ourselves from our everyday existence in order to find it. Our true life purpose is to live a sacred life by consistently expressing our spiritual values in absolutely everything we do. **A sacred life is the ongoing process of putting the energy of unconditional love into visible form by living with kind intention.**

The greatest impact we have on our world is through our daily actions, and we have countless opportunities to make positive contributions to each other every moment of every day. The seemingly small things we can do have an enormous effect on everyone around us—taking time to listen to someone in pain, smiling, telling the truth even when no one else would know the difference, honoring even the smallest of our commitments (to ourselves as well as to others), keeping a confidence, making contributions to our favorite causes, volunteering our time and effort to help the unfortunate, choosing to refrain from unkind gossip, taking time to recycle our trash—all of these things have a cumulative effect in contributing to a kinder world.

The more we become conscious of living our lives in accordance with unconditional love, the more harmonious our lives become as we express and experience the following:

- Honoring the sacredness within our own being. We are each an expression of divine love; accordingly, we treat ourselves with kindness and patience, and we honor the commitments that we make to ourselves which support our spiritual growth and our mental, emotional, and physical health.
- Accepting people as they are without trying to change them to conform to our expectations. The only way we can change others is through our own positive example.
- Feeling compassion for each other by understanding that it takes a great deal of courage for any one of us to be here.
- Realizing that no matter how unacceptable someone's behavior may seem to us, each of us is here for a reason, and we are all doing the best we can with the knowledge we have acquired and the choices we have made.

• Recognizing that we all have the same spiritual purpose —to receive and express unconditional love. We remember this in our own unique way and in our own time.

• Understanding that it is not in our greatest good to judge or criticize anyone. Since we are not in the other person's mind and feeling their experiences, we cannot possibly know how they feel or what is motivating their actions.

• Seeing life as a process of growth. There are no failures. Every situation we experience and every person we meet   is an opportunity for growth and greater insight to uni-versal truth and love.

• Respecting the fact that none of us has power over any one else. The only real power we have is within our own lives.

• Knowing that because we are all a part of the whole of existence, each one of us affects all of us. Accordingly, we take responsibility for the fact that our thoughts, words, actions, and even our underlying motivations, are impacting the entire world.

• Revering the life energy that exists within everyone and everything. Not only do we honor the sacredness in ourselves and within each other, but everything in our environment as well.

No matter how much attention we may focus on our physical nature, we are all created in the energy of unconditional love! It is important that we not confuse the unconditional love of spirit with the conditional love of the ego.

What Is Conditional Love?

Conditional love is not the same thing as the unconditional love of spirit. Unconditional love is neutral and all encompassing; whereas conditional love generally focuses on particular people. When we love someone in a conditional way (whether it is a romantic partner, spouse, ex-spouse, child, parent, friend, or acquaintance), we try to fulfill our own emotional needs by directly or indirectly manipulating them to conform to our way of thinking. Rather than accepting people as they are, we tend to want them to look, act, and think in ways that fit our own paradigms and expectations.

When we think of love in the physical sense, we may think of the warm feelings we have toward the people we like or the passionate feelings we have when we meet someone with whom we have "chemistry." The term "falling in love" is a revealing expression indicating that we sometimes lose ourselves when we are involved in a romantic relationship based on conditional love, possibly because we are looking for another person to complete us rather than looking to share our whole self. When we love in a conditional way, we try to make ourselves whole by working to make others the way we want them to be instead of working on ourselves to become more of who we are.

If we are in the habit of loving in a conditional way, we are also likely to try to fix other people's problems by telling them what to do or even doing it for them. If we become too involved, we can actually compound someone else's difficulties by superimposing ourselves into their dilemma to the point that we actually take on their same emotional issues. When we do this, we actually become victimized by the same situations that we seek to resolve.

When we love conditionally, we hold others accountable to our expectations in order to qualify for our affection. If they act the way we want them to, we express our approval; if they act contrary to our wishes, we withhold our expression of acceptance of them, usually in some form of anger. This type of thinking is based on the Perspective of Separation which polarizes our internal thought process to believe, "I am right, and you are wrong, so I think you should see things my way." As soon as we begin to judge someone as being right or wrong, it is our cue that we are not in a space of unconditional love because we are perceiving that we are the authority for someone else's life. Although we may think we pass judgment on others for all the "right" reasons, conditional love inevitably results in a power play for everyone involved because it focuses on control, which typically elicits a defensive reaction from the people whom we are trying to change. Rather than creating a climate of nurture and support, conditional love typically perpetuates an emotionally destructive environment by eroding the foundation of trust.

One of the most effective ways to open ourselves to unconditional love is to release our judgment of others. Many of us feel defensive about this statement because we say we have to make many judgments in life. Of course, we do, but perhaps we have forgotten the true meaning of the verb, "judge." Some of the definitions of *judge* that are stated in *The Merriam Webster Dictionary* are: *to form an estimate or evaluation about something; to gather information; conclude; deduce.* When viewed in this light, we can adopt a neutral, constructive perception of judgment that does not involve any form of personal attack. It is important that we remember that "judge" does *not* mean to criticize, nor does it mean that we are sanctioned to judge another human being's value as a person or to tell others how to live their lives. The energy of the intentions we project through our thoughts, words, and actions is exactly the energy we attract. When we hurt others we are not working in harmony with the energy of universal love; therefore, we hurt ourselves as well.

The bottom line is that when we practice conditional love, we are looking for others to make us feel complete. This proves to be unproductive because in order to feel whole, we have to first love ourselves.

Why Do We Have to Love Ourselves in Order to Love Someone Else Unconditionally?

We can only genuinely love and accept another without judgment by treating ourselves in the same way. The most basic human need we all have from the time we are born is to be accepted for who we truly are, including all our imperfections. If we do not address our own need to be loved unconditionally, how can we give to others that which we cannot give to ourselves?

If we want to find this kind of acceptance in our outer world, we need to first discover it within our inner personal world. Trying to express our love without being open to receiving the love of spirit is like exhaling without inhaling. We simply cannot do it without emotionally suffocating. Unconditional love is the flow of energy in all of life, and there must be a balanced exchange of energy in order to maintain the flow. Nature is a wonderful example of this—if a river does not receive water from its tributaries, it dries out. Likewise, rain is only possible because of the hydrological cycle which transforms the energy of it into evaporation, condensation, and back into rain again. Like all of nature, we are a part of a balanced cycle of energy—if we are not open to receiving, we break the flow of energy just as surely as if we are not open to giving.

Receiving energy is not the same idea as taking it. *Receiving* means opening our hearts and minds to the limitless, unconditional loving energy of the universe which is always available to all of us. *Taking* implies grasping or seizing something which is not necessarily offered to us. Spiritual love is the essence of life—we do not have to *take* it—we need only be open to receiving it.

Loving ourselves is a spiritual necessity that is greatly misunderstood in today's society in that it is many times confused with the selfish traits of narcissism. *Narcissism*, a word which evolved from the beautiful mythological Greek youth who fell in love with his own reflection, connotes vanity, self-centeredness, and insensitivity to the needs of others.

On the contrary, self-love means having the strength and courage to accept our own uniqueness, honoring and expressing our true feelings in a kind way, forgiving ourselves, and having compassion and patience with ourselves as we experience the ups and downs of life. The way we feel inside is what we radiate outside to the world. When we love and accept ourselves, we have the inner strength and energy to help others to be who they truly are, rather than trying to change them or fix their situations.

How Can We Effectively Help Others?

One of the most sensitive balancing acts we experience in our growth process is that of helping others in a way that energizes them without decreasing our own energy. There is so much suffering in the world, and most of us truly want to reach out and alleviate some of the pain—especially when we see it within our family and friends; however, unless we help others in a mindful way, we are likely to deplete ourselves by draining our own energy, rather than being a conduit for channeling the limitless energy of spirit through us and to those whom we are helping.

Odd as it may seem, we can best help others by first helping ourselves. We do this by honoring our own needs for spiritual nourishment. If we try to help someone without being in a position of emotional strength ourselves, we can quickly become drawn into someone else's drama. When this happens, not only can we not help anyone, we are actually adding to the collective pain of the world by taking on the negative issues of others. When people tell me of their pain and aggravation over complicated emotional issues in their lives, I frequently ask them, "What part of this belongs to you?" While this may seem like a surprising question, it is astonishing how often we waste our energy by getting emotionally entangled in other people's emotional dramas, rather than being a support system. Of course, we are greatly impacted by the pain of people whom we care about, and we always have our own lessons to learn or we wouldn't be involved at all. But we need to remember that we support others by reinforcing them with our strength—not by imposing our judgment on them or participating in their anger and pain.

I often think of trying to save someone by getting involved in their emotional issues as being analogous to trying to rescue a friend who has fallen into a deep hole by jumping into the hole with them. We may feel so sorry for our friend being alone in that hole that we decide we can lessen her loneliness by experiencing the situation with her, so we jump in too. When we do this, not only have we not helped our friend, we have actually added to the problem in that both of us now need assistance.

Of course, we want to help our friend, but there are other, much more effective ways by which we can accomplish this without draining anyone's energy. Let's walk through how we can help someone without jeopardizing our own well-being, using the analogy of "the hole" as an emotional crisis:

1. We need to ask our friend if she *wants* our help! So many times we waste our energy trying to change someone's situation because it is something *we* want for them, not something they want for themselves. It is pretty tough to assist someone's recovery if they are resisting us while we are doing it. For this reason, it is really important that we stay in touch with how we feel in the company of people whom we seek to help—if our energy feels drained as though we are being pulled into the hole with them, chances are they are not yet ready to take responsibility to meet us part way in helping themselves.

2. It is important to remember that there is something our friend needs to learn from falling into the hole. We each have to discover our own personal lessons that come through in the form of life's challenges. When we try to short-circuit this process for someone else, we are robbing them of an opportunity to learn something they need to know for their own spiritual growth.

3. We need to remember that the most constructive way to help someone is not to do for them, but to empower them

to do for themselves. While it is a lovely quality to be generous with our help, we are wise to remember that generosity does not mean self-sacrifice. Our friend does not need for us to save her by getting into the hole and letting her step on our back to get out. She may feel better, but we will still be stuck in the hole! What she really needs is our strength, compassion, and support so that she can get out of the hole by herself.

4. It is crucial that we remember that we can only help our friend if we stay balanced and centered ourselves. If our friend wants our help, we can stand on the outer edge of the hole and throw her a rope or invite her to reach for our hand so that we can pull her to our space of strength rather than allowing ourselves to be drawn into her pain. Similarly, we can sometimes help people to clarify their issues by suggesting options which may help them to resolve their crisis. Offering choices of solutions is not the same thing as trying to *be* the solution.

If we all subscribed to helping people by "jumping in the hole" with them and participating in their pain, eventually we would all be in the hole—which is one way of understanding how we have arrived at our present collective outside-in mentality and victim-oriented culture.

We can be of assistance to others not just by what we do, but, even more powerfully, through our own example of living in accordance with inner spiritual principles and values.
This certainly does not mean that we need to be perfect—simply that we make it our life purpose to mindfully practice choosing thoughts, words, and actions which are in accordance with the universal truth of unconditional love.

As we experience our own healing, we radiate healing energies to others through the very essence of our existence, and our judgment of others frequently transforms into a much more constructive emotion—*compassion*. When we are constantly working on healing our own lives, we resonate with the growth pains of others through our own experiences. We can therefore relate to their situations with empathy. Empathizing without judgment creates a state of grace which opens our hearts to receiving love and support from each other.

We do not need to have all the answers for people who ask our help. In fact, some times the best answer we can give is silence. It is within the silence that we express pure acceptance of another simply by listening with compassion—not to the words we are hearing with our ears—but to the feelings underneath the words we can sense with our hearts. When we do this, we empower others to access their answers from their own inner wisdom while we provide support, respect, encouragement, and objective insight.

Most importantly, we need to remember that the healing of others is not done by us but *through* us. When we tap into our universal spiritual source, we receive all the energy, love, guidance, and strength we need to help others. In fact, helping people in this way is actually energizing—not just for them, but for ourselves as well. As we draw on our spiritual center for our personal energy, there is no limit to the number of people on whom we can have a positive effect because we virtually become a channel for healing ourselves and everyone around us—even those whom we merely think about in a loving way. When we do this, we are living our lives in accordance with divine will, and we are able to focus on the light within ourselves and others even in the midst of chaos.

What Is the Light Within?

Although science has learned a great deal about light, it is still a phenomenon which remains outside of the realm of our human ability to fully comprehend—yet it is the very essence of our being.

In the scientific sense, light is the shortest vibrational wavelength and highest frequency perceivable by our human senses, giving off bursts of energy to all living matter. Unlike sound waves which need air, or water waves which need water, light waves need no support from any earth element. Light contains both electrical and magnetic radiation, which makes things visible to the human eye.

While our knowledge of light continues to expand, our scientific understanding of light gives us only a hint of its infinite nature and profound power. Light, like unconditional love, is something we can best sense with our inner awareness. The mere mention of the word *light* reminds us of many pleasant descriptions, such as: *radiant, bright, warm, delightful, floating, effortless, uplifting,* and *clear*. We seem to instinctively know that light is synonymous with our truth, as is evident in expressions such as, "It wasn't clear to me at first, but I finally saw the light." The word *enlightenment* literally means *spiritual in-sight*. When we focus on the light within ourselves and others, we are focusing on the true essence of our humanness—it is our divinity within. While love is the source of light, it is light that makes it possible for us to see the energy of universal love in physical form.

Pure light includes the full spectrum of every color known to us. When pure light passes through a prism, the prism refracts the incoming light wave into many other different wavelengths, making colors visible—violet being the shortest and red the longest. When we perceive humanity in the metaphorical sense of being one gigantic prism, we see that collectively we form a beautiful rainbow coming from one source of divine light. In effect, we are each refracting the essence of our inner core of light through the colors of our personalities. As we focus on the light within ourselves and all others, we begin to fuse into one brilliant wave of pure light as together we return to our original state of enlightenment and Oneness.

Part Two

Healing Our Past

Chapter Five

Opening to Change—Forgiveness

In order for our world to evolve to a society centered around spiritual integrity, we have to heal the past, beginning with our own personal lives.

As we discussed in Chapter Two, we can create new realities by expanding our perceptions to a higher perspective; however, the only space in time in which we are able to make choices is in the spiritual reality of the moment. More often than not, we are not functioning in the present because our minds are preoccupied with thoughts based on emotional wounds and prejudices of past relationships and experiences.

Staying focused on the past crowds the mind with negative thoughts and blocks the flow of our creative energy, resulting in stress, pain, and dis-ease. When we predominantly invest the energy of our thinking on events and people from the past, we feel stuck and powerless to change our lives—yet our human tendency is to tenaciously hold onto past behavior patterns, no matter how painful, simply because we fear change.

In this chapter we begin our personal healing process by understanding our fear of change. Once we have faced our fears, we can free ourselves from our bondage to the past through the process of *forgiveness* of ourselves and others. Forgiveness is, by far, the most powerful tool we have to release our attachment to painful associations from the past.

Isn't It Important to Remember the Past?

Past experiences serve us well when we learn from them and use these lessons as a springboard from which to launch new thought patterns that promote our health and growth. When we perceive the past as a series of universal guideposts continuously guiding us toward truth, we are acknowledging our spiritual path to wholeness.

But remembering is not the same thing as becoming entrapped in old patterns of behavior simply because we are afraid to make changes. We have an amazing propensity to hold onto the familiar—even if it is causing us harm. How often have we clung to a destructive relationship, a job we have long outgrown, or even a consistently poorly performing financial investment just because we are afraid of change? Our fear of change can be a powerful force which holds us back from evolving in our spiritual growth.

Why Do We Fear Change?

Generally speaking, our greatest fear is of the unknown. Interestingly, it isn't the actual situations we experience that cause us to feel terrified nearly so much as our fearful antici-pation of worse-case scenarios.

The changes we fear are only limited by our imagination: Fear of the lack of success and fear of success; fear of not being loved and fear of being loved; fear of losing a job and fear of staying stuck in a job; fear of not being married and fear of get-ting married; fear of not being accepted by a college and also of being accepted, and the list goes on.

Change tends to be something we want everyone else to do. If we hold to this idea, our lives become a series of "if's." If only so-and-so would be nicer to us, we would feel better; if our boss would change, we would like our jobs more; if our spouse would change, our marriages would improve. While all this may be true, it is irrelevant because we can only change ourselves. When we avoid taking responsibility for changing ourselves, we are placing virtually everyone else in charge of our lives, which is many times the very thing we fear the most.

Avoiding or denying fear only intensifies it because "what we resist, persists"; therefore, the most effective way we can handle it is by becoming aware of what we fear. When we are children, we tend to be afraid of the darkness. Interestingly, as we grow older, we are more likely to be afraid of the light because it exposes our hidden fears and invites us to deal with why we are holding onto the past. It is important to remember that feelings are transitory—we can experience fear without adopting it as our permanent reality. Like the imaginary childhood monster who disappeared when our parents turned on the light, fear dissipates when it is brought out of the shadows and into the light of awareness.

When we become adults, we can "turn on the light" for ourselves by taking an honest look at some of the rationalizations we use in order to avoid change:

• **We Want to Feel Safe**—We need to ask ourselves, safe from what? Are we really safe when we cling to the familiar? It is our spiritual nature to be the expression of perpetual growth and expansion. If we want to dwell on risk, we need to consider that the most perilous thing we can do is to forget who we are and why we are here. We are all on this earth for a reason and bring a personal expression to this physical world which absolutely no other soul can bring. We can only mindfully express our true self by being in present time. What could possibly be more safe and spiritually correct than to be who we truly are and to continue to evolve through change?

• **We Don't Have the Courage or Strength**—*Courage* (root word *cuer*, meaning *heart*) does not mean the absence of fear; indeed, we all have fears. Having courage means we have the heart to *face* our fears and to make changes for the better even when we are afraid. Does it take strength to make changes? Of course it does, but it takes a lot more of our strength to withstand the turmoil of going against the natural current of change and growth than to go with the flow of it. We are energy, and energy, by its very nature, is constant change. If we think about the times our strength has felt most depleted, has it been when we used our energy to adjust to new challenges or when we were desperately trying to stay in the same space? Whether we choose to be open to change or not, it takes courage and strength to live, so we may as well use our energy to work in harmony with the laws of nature.

- **We Want to Be Comfortable**—We need to take a reality check on this too. If we are not moving forward, we eventually become stuck in the status quo. Is it comfortable to feel stuck? Even though we may feel a little insecure moving out of familiar spaces, it is really quite healthy to experience the discomfort that comes from growth. Discomfort is caused by bumping against the boundaries of our outgrown paradigms, indicating that it is time for our mind's knowledge to catch up with our soul's wisdom. When we feel uncomfortable it is usually not because we are experiencing change, but because we are resisting it. It is like going through a growth spurt as a child—the faster our feet grew, the more often we felt the discomfort of our shoes being too tight. We certainly didn't resolve the situation by shrinking our feet—we had to create more room for our feet to grow by buying larger shoes. And so it is with change. When we feel that the world around us is beginning to close in, we can't resolve the situation by making ourselves smaller; however, we can choose to create more expansive perspectives.

- **We Don't Want to Experience Confusion**—Indeed, change does cause confusion, and what a blessing it is for us! Confusion scrambles the fixated thought patterns we have locked into so that we can rearrange them into a new system of ideas. If we think about it, the most wonderful events in our lives, such as moving to a new house, receiving a promotion, getting married, or having a baby, all create a temporary state of chaos. Eventually, things quiet down, but as we look around we see that we are in an entirely new space. Interestingly, one of the main tenets of Chaos Theory states that order resides within apparent chaos and confusion. Even though we know this at an intellectual level, we still delude ourselves by believing it is possible for us to keep the same context around all the circumstances of our lives by holding onto thought patterns from the past.

- **We Want to Avoid Pain**—In our attempt to avoid the pain of change, we many times hold onto the past. Ironically, the parts of the past to which we remain most attached are the very ones which typically elicit the most painful memories: the parent who abandoned us, the spouse who was unfaithful, the employer who cheated us, and the friend who betrayed us. Holding on to these types of memories frequently breeds self-defeating feelings of guilt and unworthiness that fuel the misperception that we are imprisoned in a life with no choices. Most of the pain we experience in our lives does not come from moving forward—it comes from holding ourselves back. Although we try hard to avoid it, pain is, in many ways, our most powerful messenger of truth.

How Does Pain Serve As a Powerful Messenger of Truth?

Perhaps the most obvious benefit to feeling pain is that it certainly gets our attention. Pain is like the indicator lights and alarms in our cars indicating something is wrong. Chances are we ignored some pretty obvious clues before the panic lights came on, such as getting gas, changing the oil, or having our battery recharged.

The same is true in our personal lives. Many times we experience mental, emotional, and physical pain only after we have ignored all the warning signs. How often do we abuse ourselves by not paying attention to the many subtle messages that come in whispers—messages to trust our intuition, relax more, exercise more, eat more nutritiously, spend more time with our families, or forgive someone? If we continue to ignore the whisper messages, the symptoms escalate until we are forced to pay attention due to a major mental, emotional, or physical crisis.

Like the indicator lights, pain is not a permanent condition in and of itself—it is a *symptom* telling us we are sensing something in our lives that is not coinciding with our inner truth. When we are living in harmony with our spiritual values, our energy is balanced and we feel at ease. When we are not living in concert with our spiritual values, our energy is out of balance and we feel pain and dis-ease.

Our bodies physically register the ease and dis-ease within our lives in a very apparent way. We can struggle with the pain as though it is the enemy or we can move to a deeper level of healing by listening to the messages that it brings. Although we have a tendency to dismiss bodily pain and illness as "just physical," in truth, they are the visible physical signals indicating deeper, underlying emotional issues calling out to be healed. Because our mind, body, and spirit are so interconnected, many times the physical symptoms we see and experience totally correlate with the emotional issues we need to resolve. For example, we may say that someone in our lives is a pain in the neck, and sure enough, we physically experience pain in our neck. Is the pain in our neck the source of the problem, or is it a relationship that needs to be resolved? We may say we are breaking our back trying to finish a project at work and soon realize that we really do have a backache. Is the pain in our back the real issue, or do we need to address a situation at work? When we refuse to forgive painful issues from our past, we may discover that our emotional constipation is confirmed by our actually experiencing physical constipation.

Likewise, when we have a serious disease, we tend to be angry with the disease as though it were the cause for our feeling ill. This is like being angry with the thermometer because it is indicating a fever—the thermometer only indicates the temperature, it does not create the fever. Like pain, disease is a messenger, not part of who we are. When we shift our focus from struggling with the disease to healing the reason for the disease, we move from being a victim to being self-empowered by perceiving the disease as a major opportunity to change our lives for the better.

Many times our greatest growth periods come through the experience of pain. Those of us who have experienced a dark time in life through serious illness or emotional trauma know the opportunity it brings for enormous wisdom and insight. Sometimes we have to experience the contrast of darkness in order to find the light. Indeed, there are lessons within our lives that may be much more apparent in the darkness of our despair because we focus more intensely when there are fewer things to see. It is like walking into a dark room—at first we can see nothing, yet after our eyes have had a chance to refocus, we begin to see particular items in the room even though the room is still dark. Likewise, we can have some very profound insights about areas of our life that need improvement while we are quietly lying in bed recovering from an illness, away from our hectic daily routines.

Painful experiences also remind us how to be compassionate and non-judgmental toward others. We can theorize about what it might feel like to have a serious sickness, deal with a drug addiction, go through a divorce, watch a friend or relative die an agonizing death, lose a job, or have serious money problems; but it is the actual experience of living through these types of painful times that opens our hearts to express tenderness and total compassion to others who are wrestling with their own challenges in life. Those of us who have attended twelve-step programs for addiction recovery for ourselves, or support groups for friends and family members of addicts, know the comfort of walking into a room of total strangers who immediately envelope us with total acceptance and unconditional love. This is because these "strangers" instantly relate to us from the heart-level of personal experience.

Pain serves many purposes, but the bottom line is that it makes us more receptive to change by alerting us to the urgent need to release something in our past that is blocking our spiritual growth.

Why Is It Essential That We Release the Past?

All the self-justifications for holding onto the past which we have been discussing are based on fear. Fear, as we know, creates separation within our personal lives and from each other. Focusing our attention and thoughts on the past stifles our growth, blocks our creative energy, creates disharmony within our lives, and freezes us in an emotional space where we cannot make new choices. When we lock into a rigid frame of mind that opposes change, we produce a state of inertia within our lives totally contrary to our spiritual nature of constant creation. The highest level of our existence is our spirit, so when we strangle our spiritual flow of energy by clutching to the past, we set the stage for mental, emotional, and physical distress. Are our lives so perfect that we want to spend all of our time on earth using our energy to resist change?

Underneath all of our pain and disease is a cry for love, and there is no greater way to open ourselves to love than to practice forgiveness. It is through forgiveness that we enable ourselves to release old fears that are inhibiting our growth and rooting us in negative past behavior patterns.

What Is Forgiveness?

Webster defines forgiving and forgive as follows: *forgiving—allowing room for error or weakness; forgive—to give up resentment of.* When we remember that we are all fallible and that the only thing we have to lose by forgiving anyone is the self-destructive resentment we are carrying, we can see more clearly that the person who benefits most from the process of forgiveness is self.

Forgiveness cleanses our minds of unhealthy thoughts which are crowding out the mental space for constructive, new thought patterns. Our society is extremely oriented to physical fitness and cleansing diets for our bodies. Yet we ignore our mental fitness and critical need to clear our minds of the toxic thoughts which we constantly recycle in our minds.

The process of forgiveness is, by far, the most powerful

tool we have to create mental clarity and inner peace. Forgiveness dissolves our emotional blockages and opens our hearts so that we can be clear to give and receive unconditional love, the basis for all healing.

We all have memories of people from the past who, living in the Perspective of Separation, have acted in ways which have caused us pain. Forgiveness does *not* mean that we are "giving in," nor does it mean that we agree with the way someone has acted toward us. When we choose to forgive, we are making a conscious decision to stop empowering the people who have hurt us by no longer allowing them to have a negative impact on our lives and control over our emotions.

As we take responsibility for our own emotional well-being we begin to see that when we say that someone "makes us feel" angry, sick, sad, or hurt, we are not being completely honest with ourselves. Because each of us can choose our own perceptions, no one can force us to feel any particular emotion—we always have the choice as to how we respond to any situation. If we choose to be an emotional sponge by absorbing the negativity and dwelling on the hurt, we are allowing someone else to have power over us. On the other hand, if we choose to learn from the situation which has caused us grief by forgiving and moving forward with greater wisdom and insight, we are truly claiming responsibility for our own feelings. This frees us to make a conscious choice to let go. "Letting go" does not mean we forget the entire experience. It means releasing the emotional knot of pain that has tied us to people whom we have not forgiven. This can hardly be considered a sacrifice, since the only thing we are letting go of is our internal bitterness and the hatred which has bonded us to the very people with whom we are angry.

No matter how long we have been storing painful memories, all the pain of the past can be released in an instant when we genuinely want to forgive. This inspiring truth is constantly verified for me through my own personal experiences and the feedback from the wonderful people who participate in the healing workshops I facilitate. A vital part of the workshop includes a forgiveness exercise, which invariably creates powerful ripple effects of healing for everyone involved. Following is a phone conversation I recently had with Elizabeth, a young woman who describes forgiveness better than is possible by any definition.

"I waited for a few weeks before I called you because I thought the 'high' I have been experiencing since the workshop might be temporary—but I realize now that it's not a high—I'm just not accustomed to feeling this light and joyful. This is the first time in my twenty-eight years of life that I wake up in the morning looking forward to the day and to sharing this joy with others. Everyone is telling me that I even look different. It's absolutely amazing—I have been in therapy analyzing my pain for fourteen years, yet I was able to let go of years and years of emotional junk pent up inside of me in a twenty-minute forgiveness exercise! You know what it's like? It's like I have had a desperate emotional thirst all of my life and suddenly my feelings are quenched. Forgiveness is about loving myself, isn't it?"

Is It Necessary to Be in the Physical Presence of Those Whom We Need to Forgive?

Of course, Elizabeth was open to forgiveness or she could not have experienced such a dramatic release so quickly; however, this is exactly the point. Even if we are still feeling hurt, the simple *intention* to forgive ourselves and others is extremely powerful. Because our thoughts are energetic impulses, we do not even have to be physically present with the person or people whom we are releasing from our bond of pain in order for them and for us to feel the energy of our healing intentions. The following story concerning a client who came to me seeking healing dramatically illustrates this point.

Carmella is thirty-five years old. A child who had been raised in a physically abusive home, she chose to discontinue having any communications with her mother when she was nineteen years old. Her mother also made no attempt to contact her over the years, even though Carmella made no secret of her location. During the sixteen years in which they had not been in touch, Carmella lived an agonized existence, going into constant rages of anger with the slightest provocation. Although she displayed a seemingly productive and successful life to the outside world, she suffered from migraine headaches, mood swings, and frequent anxiety attacks. By the time she was thirty-two years old, she discovered she had cancer. Fortunately, it was discovered early, and the chemotherapy and radiation treatments were successful in bringing her cancer into remission.

Carmella's flirt with death inspired her to pursue her healing at a deeper, spiritual level. She was aware that she was hiding a lot of anger and didn't want to wait until the next medical crisis to face some of the issues she knew were literally eating away her soul. During one of our meetings, the subject of forgiveness surfaced. Carmella said she was aware of how much she had continued to punish herself by continuing to drag her childhood issues into her adult life. She said she was willing to "try to forgive" and agreed to participate in a healing creative visualization. As she candidly put it, "Why not? I've tried everything else!"

During the visualization, I encouraged Carmella to feel kindness and respect for herself and to acknowledge her own courage and willingness to heal. As she embraced her own vulnerability and goodness, she opened up to the realization that her mother had also been a very sad child. Seeing that image enabled Carmella to feel compassion for the inner child of her mother and helped her to understand how her mother was continuing to pass on her own negative feelings to her children. In that moment Carmella reached a turning point in her life—she realized that she did not have to pass the generational baton. She stopped blaming her mother by seeing she had the power to end her own role in contributing to the long family history of perceptions steeped in abusive behavior. She chose to symbolically cut an imaginary rope that was binding both of them in mutual pain and replaced it with a circle of light around them. She sent out thoughts inviting her mother to be open to her own emotional healing.

Three days later Carmella called me and tearfully announced, "I think I have just experienced a miracle. As I left your office, I made a decision to send my mother a note. I went to the mailbox this morning to mail it, and I could not believe my eyes—there in the mailbox was a letter from my mother! She says in this letter that she had a dream three days ago that I forgave her. She says she has not stopped crying since that dream and wants to know if I could ever find it in my heart to see her again!"

Carmella saw, first hand, that she did not need to physically be with her mother in order for both of them to receive enormous positive impact from the energy of her healing thoughts. Forgiveness is not a self-sacrificing gesture; in fact, we cannot forgive another without being blessed ourselves.

If Forgiveness Is So Essential to Our Healing Process, Why Is It So Hard to Do?

One of the most frequent excuses we offer ourselves for withholding forgiveness is that we are in too much pain. We put ourselves in an emotional deadlock by waiting for our pain to disappear before we consider forgiveness. In fact, it works the other way around—our pain can only leave us when we make a conscious decision to forgive.

Children seem to find it so easy to forgive. They can have an argument and make up with each other in the blink of an eye. This is because they place a higher priority on getting back to playing happily with each other than trying to prove who is right. Perhaps the reason many adults find it so difficult to forgive is that we have forgotten what children seem to know innately—it is healthier to be peaceful and happy than it is to be self-righteous. If we feel the need to prove we are "right," we are likely to seek retribution by holding onto our anger, resentment, and hostility as though we can get even with the people who have hurt us.

The problem with this is that we, ourselves, suffer in a big way when we cling to all these unhealthy feelings. When we refuse to forgive ourselves and others, we are holding onto the energy of fear, which creates pain by blocking the flow of universal love in our lives. This wreaks havoc in our minds, attracts other angry people and situations, ruins relationships, creates discomfort in our bodies, causes diseases, and perpetuates violence and crime. As a result, we continue to hurt ourselves long after the original pain was inflicted. We also hurt others by projecting our anger onto many innocent people who happen to be in our line of fire. Ironically, in our effort to seek justice and revenge, we actually begin to act out the same aggressive behavior as the individuals who have hurt us.

We do not need to make it our personal responsibility to chastise people whom we feel have wronged us. We are each responsible for our choices; and sooner or later, whatever we project to others in the nature of our thoughts and deeds is what comes back to us. The people who hurt us will receive the natural consequences of their actions through their life experiences. If we choose to compound the hostility by seeking revenge, we will also see our own negative thoughts reflected back to us. In effect, when we withhold our forgiveness, we create a lose/lose situation.

Humanity has been graced with the gift of free will to determine how we use our personal energy, depending on the thoughts we choose. Our thoughts have the energetic capacity to heal or to hurt. Do we really want to choose thoughts which direct our divine energy to inflict pain and revenge on ourselves and others, or would we rather use our divine energy to project thoughts of love and healing into our lives and the lives of others? Our answer to this question can be the single most important factor in determining the direction and quality of our lives. When we choose thoughts of unconditional love, we are living in harmony with our spiritual integrity. When we choose thoughts of revenge and retaliation, we are, in effect, attacking ourselves just as surely as we are attacking others.

There Are So Many Forgiveness Issues
From the Past—Where Do We Begin?

Because all healing begins within, forgiveness of others begins with forgiveness of self. The way we act toward self lays the foundation for our actions toward others; so when we forgive ourselves, the pathway for forgiving others is opened as well. The issue here is not one of who is "right" and who is "wrong." It is about forgiving ourselves for holding onto self-defeating thoughts that are causing us pain. Why continue to punish ourselves every day by continuing to experience wounds of the past?

Even If We Can Forgive Ourselves, How Is It Humanly Possible to Forgive People Who Have Hurt Us Deeply?

Sometimes the actions of people who have hurt us seem so heinous and unkind that the thought of forgiving them seems like an impossible human feat. No matter how hard we try, we may feel that we cannot reconcile our feelings about them, nor understand how anyone could act so cruelly. It is only human to feel angered and upset by some of the atrocities we witness and experience in our world. What is self-destructive is not that we have these feelings—it is that we hold onto them.

It is important to remember that forgiving someone does not mean we are endorsing their harmful behavior. We do not need to feel warmly toward people who have hurt us, nor do we need to understand their actions. We may even make a healthy decision that it is not in our best interests to be in their physical presence.

Forgiveness is a form of neutral, unconditional love. When we choose to forgive someone, we are acknowledging that every single person on earth, no matter who they are or how they conduct themselves, is part of humanity and, therefore, a part of who we are. In other words, we stop looking at the objectionable physical actions of others by looking at a soul level, beneath their negative behavior. When someone behaves in a negative, manipulative way, we need to remember that they are projecting from their own reservoir of fears. The way they are treating us is exactly the way they feel about themselves. This is why self-love is so essential in that it forms the foundation for how we treat everyone around us. When we focus on someone else's negative behavior by responding the same way, we compound the problem by reinforcing their fears and our own. We then step into the darkness of the other person's world of fear, rather than bringing illumination to the situation. Instead of inviting the other person to our space of peace, we hurt ourselves by stepping into their chaos.

No matter how angry we may feel toward someone, there are no accidents; there is a reason for every single interaction we have with anyone, whether pleasant or not. They are teaching us, and we are teaching them. We can perceive even our most painful experiences as growth opportunities by asking ourselves, "What am I experiencing through this person that I need to learn?" The things that irritate us about someone else are a reflection of something we need to see within ourselves in order to mature in our spirituality. We may realize that this person is reminding us of our need to develop more self-esteem or exposing our own need to be more patient and forgiving. It could also be that we recognize that what this person is doing which is causing us pain is the same thing we have done to someone else. The important thing is that when we view our relationship issues in this way, we are learning from, rather than judging the other person. When we do this, everyone benefits.

When we withhold forgiveness and choose to ignore the messages which come to us in the form of relationships, the universe will continue to present us with people and circumstances presenting the same theme until we become aware of what we need to know. It is as though we are in a play and the same actor exits and comes back on stage again wearing a new costume. Everywhere we turn, we see the same face in a new outfit. Once we understand our message, the emotional gridlock we are experiencing generally disappears.

We can bless people who have hurt us by releasing them to the love of the universe for healing—whether we like them or not is irrelevant. When we do this we are also blessing ourselves by placing a greater priority on love and inner peace than on revenge and self-righteousness.

How Can We Send Out Thoughts of Forgiveness?

Forgiveness, like any form of thought, can be consciously chosen. While it can seem difficult at first, the more we practice forgiveness, the more natural it becomes. In fact, it actually becomes easy when we see the positive effects that forgiveness manifests in our lives. We begin to feel better about everyone—most especially ourselves!

Following is an exercise which can be used to develop and strengthen our forgiveness potential. Be patient with yourself—remember you are cultivating a new habit.

• *Clear* away your anger. Begin with a catharsis of some sort. Trying to forgive someone without first venting your feelings of pain is like trying to seal a potential volcanic eruption with a band-aid—there is usually a lot of energy that needs to be released before the wound can heal. Talk with someone who is a compassionate listener, write your feelings down on paper, or write a letter to the person you need to forgive (p.s. don't send the letter if you have used this technique simply to vent your negative feelings!). Remember, you are doing this for yourself. You deserve to be free of the pain of this situation and in charge of your own feelings.

• *Release* the need to judge who is "right" and who is "wrong." Chances are excellent that each person involved is absolutely certain he or she is right. Continuing to think this way only perpetuates more negativity and resolves nothing.

• *See* the other point of view. Remember that forgiveness is a two-way street. Forgiveness is not something we do only for others. We need to request it for our own transgressions against others as well. It is so much easier to remember who has hurt us; yet many times the best way to move away from the self-perception of being an innocent victim is to focus on the people whom you have wronged and from whom you need forgiveness.

- *Envision* whom you need to forgive and by whom you need to be forgiven as you send out kind thoughts. Forgiveness is a mutual blessing and always includes self. It need only be a simple message, such as "I release both myself and you to the infinite power of unconditional love," or "As I focus on my own light within, I also see the light within you."

- *Persist* through negative thoughts. Any time a negative thought about a person recurs, immediately say something in your internal dialogue to defuse the negativity, such as "I release these negative thoughts and see that we experience peaceful resolution" or, "I surrender my thoughts to the source of love and light." If necessary, repeat it like a mantra to reinforce your intention of forgiveness.

- *Shift* your intentions. It does not matter if, at first, your intentions are kinder than your feelings. Thought precedes form. As you shift your intentions, the energy of forgiveness will manifest in your physical reality. Since unconditional love is the most powerful energy in existence, eventually you will come to believe and experience the feelings of what you are saying because you are working in harmony with divine will.

- *Choose* to continue sending thoughts of kindness. By doing so, you immeasurably increase your capacity to receive the limitless blessings of love in your own life.

- *Expect* a healing to occur in a way that is for the good of all and in perfect accord with divine will.

When we cultivate an attitude of forgiveness, we are making a personal contribution to the healing of the world. Forgiveness is also the greatest gift we can ever give to ourselves because it frees us to choose new perceptions which are based on unconditional love.

Chapter Six

Becoming Aware of
Our Basic Beliefs

When we are no longer blinded by our emotional wounds of the past, we are free to move onto the next step in healing our past: becoming aware of our subconscious basic beliefs. Our basic beliefs are the fundamental concepts we have formed about ourselves and the world around us, based on the mental input we have received throughout our lives. They are the underlying thought forms deep within our psyche that support all our views of life. Our basic beliefs have profound impact on the quality of our lives because they are the core of personal values governing absolutely every perception we choose.

Many of our basic beliefs generate self-limiting thoughts because they are framed within our childhood Perspective of Separation, rooted in societal training, and do not reflect our whole self. Before we can choose new perceptions based on Oneness and unconditional love, we need to first become totally conscious of what our subconscious basic beliefs are, where they originated, and why we are holding onto them. If we bought new furniture for our homes, we wouldn't place all the new furniture in the same places with the old furniture— we would clean out the old to create space for the new. The same is true for our minds. We need to sort out which of our basic beliefs we have outgrown in order to create the mental space for new, more expanded perceptions that coincide with our spiritual truth.

Where Do Our Basic Beliefs Originate?

Beginning early in our childhoods, we are mentally pro-grammed with a central system of beliefs influenced by many years of social conditioning, religious doctrines, family struc-ture, teaching institutions, and customs. When we were very young children, we did not have the mental capabilities to screen what was our personal truth and what was someone else's, so we unconditionally accepted the perceptions of our parents and people around us as absolute truth. If a parent consistently scolded us by saying we were bad or a teacher in kindergarten told us we were not bright, we most likely accepted these statements as gospel.

Our minds are like computers recording every single thought and experience we have ever had into the limitless storage of our subconscious. As a result, our childhood per-ceptions permeate deeply into our subconscious, and we unconsciously continue to carry both the positive and nega-tive messages into adulthood.

Why Do We Need to Know Our Basic Beliefs?

The problem with unconditionally accepting all our childhood mental tapes is that our lives change as we mature. Even though many of our basic beliefs are no longer appro-priate for us, we frequently allow them to rule our lives long after they are relevant. This is a bit like continuing to believe in the tooth fairy at the age of forty and still expecting to find money beneath our pillow. At the age of four, it fit our para-digms to believe that a mysterious visitor would tiptoe into our bedroom at night and transform a tooth into money—at the age of forty we have hopefully updated our version of the tooth fairy to coincide with a more mature point of view.

While we naturally outgrow the more obvious juvenile paradigms, there are countless other, more subtle, childhood beliefs which can continue to haunt us even though we may not be aware of them. The childhood message "big boys don't cry" may unconsciously amplify into the emotionally repressive adult connotation, "it is not acceptable for a grown man to express his emotions." "Money is dirty" is good advice to a toddler who is about to put a dollar bill into his mouth but this subconscious message could generate some very negative adult perceptions about wealth and money. "You have to do all your work before you can play" can plant the seeds for an adult workaholic who can't seem to justify taking time to relax and have fun. "Don't ever be selfish" can grow into a guilt-producing adult perception which implies it is selfish to nurture ourselves. And the quick reaction of an angry parent saying "you are bad" to a mischievous child can breed very painful adult feelings of unworthiness.

Unless we make a concerted effort to become aware of our basic beliefs and where they came from, we can unknowingly base our entire lifetime on a foundation of "tooth fairy ideas." As a result, these same old childhood tapes can continue to trigger automatic responses without our ever understanding why we react to people and situations the way we do. This is called unconscious living because all of our energy is spent blindly reacting rather than living pro-actively from a space of conscious awareness of our own personal truth.

Blaming the people from our childhood who imparted these negative messages is a waste of our energy and only serves to make us feel even more powerless and victimized. Our parents and caretakers can justify the beliefs they passed on to us by saying their parents passed the same ones onto them. We can all continue to play this game of living backwards by pointing an accusing finger at the generation preceding us, but what is the point? **Do we need to find someone to blame or do we want to stop our suffering?** If we genuinely want to heal ourselves and become whole, we need to slam on the emotional brakes and announce to ourselves, "the buck stops right here and now with me!"

Living consciously requires us to move into the present time and make it our personal responsibility to develop adult perceptions that correlate with our adult values. When a farmer wants to plant a new crop, he cultivates his field to awaken the natural potential of the soil to nourish new seeds. Likewise, we can cultivate the potential for new perspectives by bringing our subconscious beliefs up to the surface of our consciousness. This allows us to plant the seeds of new thoughts (basic beliefs) which support the outcomes we want to create.

Choosing new perceptions without having coinciding subconscious beliefs to support them is as shallow and ineffective as trying to grow a new plant with no roots—there is no way it can take hold. For example, if we want to be financially prosperous but have an underlying core belief that we are not worthy of success, one thought cancels out the other, and nothing will change. We have to first choose to reprogram our minds to believe we are worthy of success in order to plant the seeds of thinking that nourish and support our new perceptions of financial abundance.

Updating our basic beliefs is an extremely powerful way to transform our lives. Because our feelings are the expression of our soul, healing our emotional issues works at the deepest level of our being—the spiritual level. Emotional healing creates a core of spiritual wholeness within us that automatically radiates the energy of health and well-being into our mental and physical levels of existence as well.

How Can We Become Conscious of Which Basic Beliefs Are Blocking Our Potential?

It would be wonderful if we established a social custom to bridge puberty and adulthood with a spiritual retreat—a sacred period of time when we could sanction ourselves to sort out which of our childhood beliefs are truly our own and which ones are someone else's emotional hand-me-downs.

In the absence of this luxury, we need to create the time to make a conscious assessment of the subliminal principles to which we have subscribed and how they affect our overall views of life. As adults, we have the capacity to discern which of the basic beliefs we are storing in our memory bank are healthy ones that are in our greatest good and which ones we choose to change.

Following is a Self-Evaluation of the Basic Beliefs Underlying Our Perceptions Of Life. This is a summary of seven major areas in which we anchor our perceptions about self and our relationship to the world: Self-Worth, Self-Responsibility, Attitude, Inner Power, Commitment, Openness To Change, and Trust In The Universe.

We can become aware of our beliefs in each of these areas by scanning the questions within each of the belief areas and asking ourselves, "Do I relate to the statements of separation or to the statements of Oneness?" The statements of separation correspond with fear and lock us into self-defeating behaviors, while the statements of Oneness resonate with our spiritual truth of unconditional universal love and open us to our greater potential.

Although an honest self-assessment may reveal it is in our greatest good to adjust our outlook in all seven areas, there are usually one or two prevalent ones which jump to our attention. It is best to trust our immediate, spontaneous responses to these questions.

When we analyze ourselves and deliberate over the answers, we run the risk of falling into the trap of self-judgment rather than pure awareness.

Since our beliefs in all of these areas are interdependent, we can be inspired by the fact that when we heal the one or two priority issues which are blocking our potential, all the others are also positively affected. Like a house of cards, when we remove the major fear supporting many other perceptions of separation, they all begin to fall.

Remember, this evaluation is not an exercise in self-criticism, nor does it involve judgment of others. It is merely a tool to shed the light of self-awareness on the foundation of beliefs upon which we base our viewpoints of life.

SELF-EVALUATION

BASIC BELIEFS UNDERLYING OUR PERCEPTIONS OF LIFE

1. **SELF-WORTH**
   Do I love myself?
   Do I believe that I deserve to be loved, healthy, happy, and successful?

   Oneness   Realizing that unconditional love begins with self; feeling worthy of life's blessings; treating oneself with compassion and kindness; being open to receiving the loving energy of the universe; taking the time to go inside of self for spiritual regeneration.

   Separation   Feeling a sense of non-entitlement to the blessings of life; compulsively reacting to external demands; not acknowledging the need to recharge; looking to others for approval and validation; feeling responsible for the happiness of others.

2. **SELF-RESPONSIBILITY**
   Do I believe that my personal reality is a reflection of my thoughts and actions?
   Do I believe I am responsible for choosing perceptions that are in alignment with my spiritual truth?

   Oneness   Living from the inside-out; taking responsibility for the perceptions that create our personal reality; using personal energy to pro-actively create perceptions based on inner spiritual truth; acknowledging challenges in life as spiritual growth opportunities.

Separation   Living from the outside-in; feeling like a victim; using personal energy to react to outer circumstances; blaming others for the circumstances and quality of one's life; holding other people responsible for one's happiness and fulfillment.

3.   **ATTITUDE**
What is my outlook on life in general?

Oneness   Having a positive attitude rooted in spiritual strength; leaving space for optimistic outcomes; seeing life as a process of learning and growth; viewing life with imagination and enthusiasm.

Separation   Having a negative attitude; expecting the worst; viewing life as a difficult "win/lose" competitive event; feeling life has to be hard; a survival attitude.

4.   **INNER POWER**
Do I believe that I have the power to create changes within my life, based on the perceptions I choose?

Oneness   Having awareness and profound respect for one's ability to direct divine energy through the power of thought; believing in personal inner power to create changes within one's personal reality.

Separation   Believing that one does not have the power to choose personal perceptions and that thoughts and actions have no energy or impact on anyone; or the other side of the coin, believing one has the power to change other people.

5. **COMMITMENT**
    Am I committed to sharing the gift of who I am with the world by expressing my true self and my unique talents?

    Oneness   Having the courage to express one's unique and true self; being open and honest; being willing to enthusiastically share the gift of one's self with the world.

    Separation   Holding back on one's creative potential and true expression of feelings; being emotionally armored; being a perfectionist; judging self harshly.

6. **OPENNESS TO CHANGE**
    Am I flexible and willing to go with the constant flow of changes within my life?

    Oneness   Greeting life with fluidity by choosing to be in the present; seeing life as a process of change and growth; having the courage to make decisions; being open to new opportunities and situations; going with the flow of life events.

    Separation   Resisting the flow of life; being stuck in the guilt of the past and the fear of the future; afraid to make decisions; trying to make life so secure so as to avoid having to face new challenges; waiting for changes to happen *to* us.

7. **TRUST IN THE UNIVERSE**
    Do I believe that I am supported by a higher spiritual reality that transcends the realm of our physical world?

    Oneness   Believing in a personal spiritual connection with a divine field of unconditional love and light beyond our human, physical existence; trusting that the universe is supportive when one is in alignment with spiritual truth; believing in an intuitive inner knowing that is connected to a field of universal intelligence.

Separation   Feeling that we are all separate from each other and from our outer existence; viewing one's human potential as being limited to the physical plane of existence; believing that what is apparent to one's physical eyes is all there is to reality; believing something can only be real if proven by logical concepts.

In order to uncover the areas in which we need to heal, we can ask ourselves the following questions about this self-evaluation:

In which areas did I discover my beliefs are rooted in separation?

Are there one or two areas which immediately jumped out as a priority issue(s)?

Where does this belief(s) come from? (i.e. parents, family culture, religion)

Is this my own personal truth now that I am an adult?

DO I CHOOSE TO CHANGE THIS BELIEF(S)?

Doing this evaluation may help us to uncover the startling fact that, for most of our lives, we have been acting from a core of beliefs that are not our adult truth. For example, we may discover that one of our growth issues is Self-Worth and realize that we are still engaged in the childhood game of desperately trying to gain the approval of our parents or that the beliefs we carry from our religious upbringing are still perpetuating chronic feelings of guilt.

Once we are aware of which basic beliefs are fear based, we have a choice—do we want to continue living the same patterns or do we choose to open ourselves to greater potential? Whatever our self-limiting issues may be, we have the inner power to transform our lives by expanding our personal basic beliefs to coincide with our spiritual truth of Oneness and unconditional love. (We discuss how to do this in Chapter Seven.)

We may discover that we have been holding onto many of our basic beliefs since childhood, whether or not they have been in our greatest good. Before we can release outgrown beliefs and replace them with perceptions based on Oneness, we need to take a close look at how our old paradigms have been supporting negative emotional patterns which may be sabotaging our potential. Once we understand not only what our basic beliefs are but what effect they have on the quality of our lives, we can consciously choose to transform our beliefs which are based on fear and separation into new ones which are aligned with The Perspective of Oneness.

Why Do We Hold onto Self-Defeating Basic Beliefs?

Many times we deliberately hinder our capacity to experience success and happiness by holding onto counter-productive beliefs and behaviors. When we do this, we are sabotaging ourselves. To state this in a more spiritual context—we are more frightened of the brilliant light of our unlimited potential than we are of the lack of success. If this seems hard to believe, think about decisions we have made to fulfill other people's expectations even when we know, at a gut level, it is not in our own greatest good. We make these self-sabotaging decisions because we are reacting from a set of beliefs that are not based on our own values. This behavior usually creates situations which cause us great unhappiness, such as:

A highly intuitive teenager finds she has a gift to write beautiful poems and stories. She feels fulfilled and in her correct space as the insights and stories flow effortlessly from her mind through the pen. In her junior year of college, she undermines her natural talent by switching her major to computer science; not because she wants to, but because she has an underlying fear that she will never be good enough to make a living utilizing her writing skills.

A young father discovers he truly prefers staying home and caring for his two young children to the job he presently has as an office manager. He and his wife agree they will both be more happy if he stays home full time and she pursues her career as a school teacher. At the last minute, he changes his mind because he is afraid he will be criticized by others because he does not fit the traditional male role model of society.

We act out our self-defeating basic beliefs through a myriad of intriguing sabotaging behaviors. These negative thought patterns have one thing in common: *they focus on our wounds rather than on our wellness.* Remember, what we focus on creates more of the same. As a result, we can end up building our entire life on the theme of our pain rather than on our healing. Our emotional recovery and spiritual well-being depend on whether we are willing to face the truth: No matter how hard we try to wriggle out of admitting it, we are getting some form of emotional gratification when we stay invested in negative thought patterns. Perhaps it is to elicit attention, sympathy, or praise. Whatever the justification, once we understand our underlying motivations and recognize how we are hurting ourselves, we can then find healthier ways to support our emotional needs.

The following pages describe some examples of the self-sabotaging roles we play that keep us stuck in unhealthy belief systems. These behavioral descriptions illustrate some of the ways we act out our perceptions that are rooted in separation. The roles correlate with the belief systems outlined in the self-evaluation just completed. Although these are typical examples, we need to recognize that each of us has our own ingenious style of playing out these self-defeating behaviors.

Even though most of us have played every one of these roles at one time or another in our lives, the important thing is to focus on the one or two priority separation issues which became apparent to you when doing the self-assessment of your belief systems.

Again, the intention of this self-assessment is to tweak our self-awareness, so it is important that we adopt an attitude of compassion, gentleness, and humor about ourselves as we read through these self-saboteur roles. These roles are behaviors—not labels of who we truly are. None of us is permanently cast into any role in life. These are simply frames of mind that can be changed through awareness and choice.

SELF-SABOTAGING BEHAVIORS

(SEVEN WAYS TO STAY STUCK IN OUR EMOTIONAL PAIN)

1. **The Martyr Role (Basic Belief Issue—Self Worth)**
    This is a syndrome in which we have difficulty acknowledging our own worthiness to receive. Our lives feel out of balance as we attempt to satisfy everyone else's needs, even if it means sacrificing our own. We especially tend to get locked into this role if we have been raised in an environment which has taught us that it is selfish to nurture ourselves. Because we do not feel entitled to our own sense of value, we try to validate our worth through the eyes of other people. We have difficulty saying "no," so we many times allow our time and energy to be beholden to other people's beck and call. As a result, we feel resentful, overburdened, and unappreciated. If we do not understand the importance of honoring our own needs, we tend to drive ourselves into the ground with self-depleting behaviors such as overworking, overeating, and over committing ourselves in general. We don't stop until we get sick or disabled in some way, which is the only time we

feel entitled to be gentle with ourselves. The emotional buy-in to this behavior is that we tell ourselves, "See what a good person I am—I am always giving to others." While giving to others is a virtuous and essential human quality, perhaps what we are forgetting is that loving others begins with loving ourselves. We don't need to prove ourselves to anyone in order to qualify for universal love—each of us is worthy of receiving it simply because we exist. We deserve and need to regularly create quiet, personal time and space to regenerate ourselves by being open to receiving the loving energy of the universe. When we do this, we become a conduit for limitless energy which blesses and renews us individually, as well as everyone around us.

2.   The Victim Role (Basic Belief Issue—Self-Responsibility)
    This role tends to be melodramatic, filled with wild and crazy emotional ups and downs. We actually begin to believe that we have no responsibility for all the bad things that have happened to us and for all the "mean people" we have had to deal with. This is a role of playing helpless, and involves a great deal of blaming because we want to pretend that other people are responsible for the situations in our lives. If only we weren't so hurt, so poor, so sick, so tired, we could gain control of our lives. The irony is that as soon as things begin to settle down, we are already set with the emotional ingredients to perpetuate the next drama. There is a definite emotional payoff to this role because we can pull lots of other people into our drama as we assign our friends and family members things they can do to make us feel better and to fulfill our needs. We can become so self-absorbed with our wounds that we become oblivious to anyone else's need for a compassionate friend. Whether consciously or not, we use this role to gain center stage in seeking attention. We justify this behavior with the implied message, "It's not my fault that things have worked out so poorly." The circumstances in our lives are not punishments—they are opportunities for growth. Instead of, "why me?" we need to ask ourselves, "what is it that I need to learn from this person or situation?" As we

learn to gracefully acknowledge that whatever we are experiencing is directly related to our perspective of life and the perceptions we are choosing, we transition from playing victim to being an active participant in our own lives.

3.   The Pessimist Role (Basic Belief Issue—Attitude)

This is an emotional niche which specializes in focusing on problems rather than resolutions. When we play this role, we like to concentrate on what is wrong about life which, given this perspective, is potentially everything. We can be sure that our bleak philosophy of life will be consistently validated because when our thinking is negative, we attract exactly the same energy. We make it a practice to anticipate problems in everything we do and, lo and behold, we encounter the very difficulties we imagined. Mission accomplished: We can now make the "I told you so" announcement to those who are strong enough to hang around us. This is a role where we also get to impact many other people because not only do we view our own lives as a futile attempt to endure life's challenges; but we also feel compelled to point this out to everyone else about their lives. It takes a lot of energy to play this role because we have to convert everything in life to its negative aspect. It's like getting a roll of film developed, throwing out the pictures, and saving only the negatives. We have to squint and struggle to see anything because we are looking at only the shadow images of the true pictures. We justify this behavior by choosing to believe we can avoid disappointments by dealing with all the negatives up front. We are so prepared for failure and disappointment, we squeeze out the space for success and joy. What could be more disappointing than seeing our worst expectations consistently coming true? Wouldn't it be a lot more productive and enjoyable, as well as take a lot less energy, to look at life from the positive side?

4.   The Controller Role (Basic Belief Issue—Personal Power)

When we play this role we delude ourselves into thinking that we change our own lives by exercising power over other people. Depending on our personalities, we function in a subtle way through criticism and judgment or, more aggressively, through overt attack and intimidation. Rather than work on ourselves, we become self-appointed experts for whomever we think we can "fix," as though we believe they need to measure their accomplishments by our standards. When we play this role, we find ourselves wielding that mean, little "should" word all over the place. Whether it's about a hairstyle, what to eat, how to raise kids or make more money, we've got *their* answers! But really, we don't have anyone else's answers except our own. Although we play this role under the guise of caring, if we truly want to help someone, one of the most effective things we can do is to enable them to discover their own resolutions by listening compassionately and without judgment. The emotional dividend of playing the Controller is that we get to say, "I'm telling you this for your own good." Are we really, or are we attempting to complete our lives by trying to control others rather than working on our own issues of personal growth? Our power is *within*, not over anyone else—the only person we have the personal power to change is ourselves.

5. The Perfectionist Role (Basic Belief Issue—Commitment)

One very effective way to play self-defeating games with ourselves is to be a perfectionist. When we are playing this role, we are afraid to act upon our intuitive feelings and ideas because we feel too vulnerable. We don't commit ourselves to sincerely expressing ourselves or unleashing our talents until we are sure that all the factors which could possibly contribute to failure (or to being criticized by others) are eradicated. We refuse to even start taking piano lessons unless we are sure we will sound like Beethoven on our first attempt. By demanding perfection of ourselves, we give ourselves the ideal excuse not to try anything that requires exposing our true self. Demanding that we be perfect is a form of self-attack in which we focus on our flaws. We frequently say that other people are never satisfied with our best efforts. In truth, we constantly undermine our own value by becoming a master of self-criticism.

This becomes a blanket justification for not fulfilling our potential because we perceive that we are never quite good enough or qualified enough to shine at anything. The emotional buy-in is that we justify our avoidance of commitment by saying, "There is no use in trying—I'm not good enough to really succeed at anything." Sure enough, our fears are reinforced and we do not succeed at most things—not because we can't, but simply because we don't really commit ourselves to sharing our genuine self with the world. Withholding the expression of our true self is a behavior which causes us pain at every level because we are constantly in a state of contraction. We need be gentle with ourselves by remembering that none of us is perfect. Our purpose on earth is to expand our spiritual growth by exploring and expressing the many glorious facets of ourselves.

6. **The Resister Role (Basic Belief Issue—Openness to Change)**
    Another sure way to limit our potential is to resist the flow of change in our lives. This is a very self-deluding perception because the process of change is the essence of life—we can participate in it or we can just let it happen to us. When we absolutely have to change the direction of our lives, as in the case of being fired from a job, our opposition is strong enough to leave a trail of skid marks behind us. Life becomes a waiting game. It is like hiding in a closet and waiting for a guarantee that everything will be forever safe outside before we agree to come out. When we play this role, we are saving up our lives for retirement; and chances are that when it comes, we will feel too old, too poor, and/or too tired to make any changes. We dance back and forth between the past and the future, believing it is either too soon or too late to write a book, go to college, change jobs, get married, buy a house, have children, sign up for yoga classes, take dance lessons, go on a trip, or learn a foreign language. Sadly, the one place in time in which we are totally absent is the only time that is real—the present. The emotional dividend here is that we get to say, "I didn't make the wrong choice." But is this true? Is there anything more painful than being stuck in the past and feeling helpless to make changes? When we are in the present, we can always create new possibilities by choosing new perceptions.

7. **The Skeptic Role (Basic Belief Issue—Trust in the Universe)**

This is a role of not trusting in a spiritual power beyond our material world because we believe that unless something can be perceived by our physical senses, it cannot exist. This belief system, centering on self as an independent entity, isolates our mind and body from our higher spiritual self. Believing that we are separate within ourselves, we also feel separated and disconnected from our fellow humans and our entire environment. If we do not believe in our connection to a higher universal wisdom, we are unable to trust our right-brain intuitive thinking. As a result, we become locked into left-brain paradigms and try to control others by demanding they substantiate their ideas, insights, and philosophies to accommodate our limited, logical perspective on life. Since we do not believe we can call upon a Supreme Being to regenerate ourselves, we look to other people to inspire us and replenish our energy. Not surprisingly, it can be exhausting to be around someone who is functioning in this role. The rationalization we use for holding onto this belief is that we claim it is naive and weak to believe that we can trust in a benevolent spiritual energy beyond our physical existence to provide us with loving support. We need to ask ourselves, "Is this philosophy of life perpetuating joy, harmony, peace, and love within our lives?" Where do we find our source of renewal and inspiration?

After doing this exercise, some of us may be feeling a twinge of self-justification. We might feel entitled to exhibit any or all of these pain behaviors because of having been hurt many times. One could say, "Of course, I act like a victim!—you would too if your house were robbed, your car died, and you lost your job all in the same year like I have." Certainly, these are the types of situations that hurt our feelings. Feelings require no explanation—they simply are what they are and, accordingly, deserve honest expression.

Evaluating the reasons we feel the way we do is a vital step in our emotional recovery; however, we get caught in our own trap of self-despair if we endlessly analyze all the reasons we are holding onto our negative emotional patterns. When we continue to do this, eventually we feel paralyzed. We feel split in half, and we threaten an emotional strike because the two sides of our brain are in a stand-off: Our right-brain says, "If you want to change your life, change your perspective."

And the other half argues, "Oh yeah? Well I'll change my outlook on life when my situation gets better."

Round and round we go and, like a labor strike, if we cannot reach an internal agreement, there will be a shut-down. How many times have we emotionally shut down because we got so caught up in analyzing and rationalizing our individual dramas that we failed to see the larger life view? At some point we need to decide that we have sufficient information and awareness to make a conscious choice to move on to a higher perspective.

As we evolve in our spiritual growth, we can rise above our day-to-day traumas and see a much broader overview of the emotional patterns in our life experiences. As we rise to this observer role, we begin to see that the universe provides us with a tailor-made curriculum designed to specifically chal-lenge the areas in which we most need to grow. For example, if we are constantly surrounded by people whom we perceive to be domineering and controlling, perhaps we are accommo-dating them by engaging in the victim role syndrome; or if we sense that we are always struggling to experience abundance in our lives, maybe we need to address the fact that we have been playing the self-less "I'm not worthy of goodness" role.

When we are ready to let go of our self-sabotaging behav-iors, we can literally reprogram one or all of our basic beliefs to move from perceptions of fear and separation to perceptions rooted in self-love and the truth of our Oneness with the uni-verse. We accomplish this through the process of affirmations.

Chapter Seven

Choosing Basic Beliefs of Oneness

When we become conscious of our self-limiting belief systems, as well as our self-sabotaging behaviors, we move out of the obscurity of the past and into the light of the present where we are free to reprogram our minds with new beliefs that reflect our personal truth and spiritual values. We can transform our fearful beliefs rooted in the Perspective of Separation to beliefs based on the Perspective of Oneness, the essence of which is unconditional love for self and others. We empower ourselves to do this through *affirmations*.

Affirmations are positive self-statements we consciously choose to confirm our goodness and truth. Because words have energy, affirmations are very effective in accomplishing several purposes:

- They neutralize our self-doubts;
- They retrain our thinking to focus on our spiritual strength and wholeness;
- They push us beyond our paradigms; and
- Most importantly, they reprogram our basic beliefs by transforming the energy of our fears into the energy of universal love, beginning with love and respect for self.

Why Are Affirmations So Effective at Reprogramming Our Basic Beliefs?

Whether we realize it or not, we have a constant dialogue going on inside of our heads. The words we choose in our self-talk have tremendous impact on our feelings because words have creative energy. When we say positive things to ourselves, we feel energized and self-supported; and when we say negative things to ourselves, our energy level drops and we feel self-attacked.

Our minds are like computers in that they store every single thought, word, and experience we have ever had in our subconscious. The messages we store in our subconscious determine how we feel about life. If we program a lot of words with negative energy into our subconscious computer, we feel poorly about ourselves and others; if we program a lot of words with positive energy into our subconscious computer, we feel good about ourselves and the world around us.

Our subconscious computer has no sense of humor and does not discern what is truth and what is not—it records everything verbatim. For example, if we frequently tell ourselves that we are loving and kind, that is exactly the message it stores. If, on the other hand, we consistently tell ourselves that we are losers, that is also exactly the message that is stored. The only thing that filters what goes into our subconscious is the power of our conscious mind to choose the thoughts we think and the words we speak. When we begin to truly realize this, we develop a profound respect for the importance of choosing our thoughts and words with great care.

If we want to change our beliefs, we need to change how we talk to ourselves. The process of using affirmations is self-empowering because it enables us to reprogram our subconscious beliefs by putting conscious positive messages into our subconscious storage. Using the computer analogy, we can take the basic beliefs which we brought up to the conscious level, and if we decide we no longer want to store these perceptions, we can symbolically push the "delete" button. This is essentially what we did when we went through the mental housecleaning in the previous chapter. We can now reprogram our minds with healing words that integrate our minds and bodies with our spiritual truth. The way we feel about ourselves lays the foundation for all of our perceptions about our outer world, so the most powerful way to change all of our basic beliefs is to begin at the level of self.

One very important point:

We Do *Not* Have to Believe Our Affirmations Before We Say Them.

Actually, it works the other way around . . .

In Order to Change What We Believe, We Have to *First* Change How We Talk To Ourselves—Our Beliefs Will Follow.

This is certainly not a new idea. Every belief we have is the result of words and thoughts that have been repeated to us countless times in countless ways. It's just that most of the time we have allowed these messages to be filed into our subconscious memory without consciously screening them. When we state affirmations to ourselves, we are consciously choosing to store the thoughts and words which coincide with our own personal beliefs, not someone else's. If we want to change what we believe, we have to change what we say to ourselves. Self-dialogue has a hypnotic effect—when we tell ourselves something often enough, we will come to believe it. Perhaps one of the best examples of this is Muhammad Ali. When he was a relatively unknown fighter named Cassius Clay, he constantly announced a simple, but very powerful, affirmation to the press and anyone else who would listen to him: "I am the greatest." Eventually his affirmation grew into his reality, and he became one of the greatest boxers in history!

How Do We Construct Powerful and Effective Affirmations?

There are certain essential factors that are necessary in order to create effective affirmations that work in accordance with the dynamic principles of thought. Following are some essential components for constructing powerful affirmations which can turn around our basic beliefs. Affirmations need to include the 'Six P's', as follows:

Personal—It cannot be said too often—we can only change *ourselves*. We can quite effectively affirm, "I am a happy, positive person" and confidently expect to see a shift in our attitude; however, if our affirmation is, "Harry is a happy man," have we really made a dent in Harry's attitude? When we change our own perceptions we do, however, have an effect on Harry and everyone else because we are projecting a positive energy. What we send out is what comes back to us!

Present Tense—The only space in time in which we have a choice to change our perceptions is in the present. We can only affirm a new course of action in the present because yesterday has already passed, and tomorrow has not yet happened. Including words in an affirmation such as, "I will, I want to, and I wish I had" are therefore totally ineffective because they create a situation of wanting or wishing, not the desired result. Words that announce "I AM, I NOW SEE, I AFFIRM, and I CHOOSE" are extremely powerful because they declare our inner power to change our personal reality in this very moment by the way in which we are consciously choosing to direct the energy of our words.

Precise Intention—We are responsible for the words we use because words are energy, and energy creates physical reality. Yet we tend to grossly underestimate the impact of what we say. Most of us have experienced situations where we have been on the receiving end of people hurling cruel words at us in a fit of anger, only to be followed by their saying, "Hey, I didn't mean what I said." Perhaps they didn't, but the negative energy behind their words felt as real as if they had stabbed us in the heart. Affirmations create a physical reality—it is imperative that what we are saying is what we truly want to create. As the saying goes, "Be careful what you wish for because it might come true."

Positive—The word affirm means to assert positively. Positive statements are self-affirming, self-empowering, and inspiring. Positive self-statements may initially feel strange because, sad as it is, most of us find it easier to be self-critical than to say good things about ourselves. The subconscious mind is like a tape recorder and does not interpret the irony of a negative statement. It simply stores the words. For example: If our affirmation is, "I am not angry and upset," which words are we focusing on? Chances are, we are clinging to "angry and upset." Is this self-empowering and inspiring? For this reason, it is important that we avoid using words that carry negative energy and self-judgment, such as: *can't, won't, should, shouldn't.* There is an old expression in the computer industry, "garbage in, garbage out" which calls attention to the need for quality programming if we expect quality results. Our subconscious mind feeds back to us the words and thoughts we have programmed into it. If we expect to reap positive results, we need to sow positive seeds of thought.

Potential–Infinite—Dare to affirm new realities without worrying about the "how" it will happen. Surrendering the outcome to the Universe is the magic that creates the space for our dreams to come true in ways that transcend our human design.

Passionate—Dare to feel your new affirmations in your heart. It doesn't matter whether you believe what you are affirming – you will come to believe what you are saying. Passion is the soul's motivation to expand your perceptions.

Remember To:

Be Brief—Affirmations stimulate us by sparking our motivation to change our behavior. If we make them complicated and lengthy, we are likely to bore ourselves and not want to work with them.

Repeat As Often As Necessary—Our new seeds of thought need some time to germinate in order for the roots of new beliefs to take hold. It took us a lifetime to obtain our negative belief systems. If we want to reprogram our thinking, it is only reasonable that we have to repeat our affirmations for a while until we believe them. We can do this by saying them aloud, repeating them to ourselves in a mirror, and mindfully including them in conversations with others. Another easy and very effective technique is to record them on tape in our own voice. There is something very convincing about hearing our own voice giving us positive, affirming statements about who we are. We can play the tape back at any time, but listening to our affirmations before sleep is the best time because we are slipping into our subconscious state which, as we discussed, is accepting of any message we give to it, without discernment.

The length of time we need to repeat affirmations varies for each individual depending on our stage of growth. It may be a few times for some and a lot more often for others. Affirmations are declarations of our true spiritual nature to be creative, positive, and whole. Because we recognize this as our truth at a soul level, moving onto our chosen new perceptions tends to embed itself into our subconscious very quickly.

How Do We Transform Our Feelings of Separation into Affirmations of Oneness?

In order to understand how we can transform our feelings of separation into affirmations of Oneness, it is important that we recognize the difference between the energy of the words *feel* and *am*. Feelings are personal sensations which are variable and transitory. *Are* and *am* are proclamations of truth which are consistent and in accordance with the principles of the universe. Affirmations nourish our souls by reminding us of who we truly *are*. We can feel whatever we want to feel, think however we want to think, and act however we want to act; however, none of these things can change universal truth. For example: we can feel annoyed, angry, sad, happy, or pleased with our mother at different times in our lives; but no matter what our feelings, it does not change the truth that we are her child.

Without a doubt, the most important affirmation we can ever repeat to ourselves (and we can never repeat it too often) is "I AM LOVE," because lack of self-love is at the root of all of our perceptions of separation.

Remember, affirmations do not change who we are. Repeating affirmations is like wiping the fog off the mirror—they just allow us to see our true spiritual self more clearly. Even though at times we may not feel that we are worthy of love, it does not change the universal truth that all of us, at the core of our being, are the essence of unconditional divine love.

The following few pages contain some examples of how we can transform our self-scaring feelings of separation based on fear to self-*caring* affirmations of Oneness based on love. Again, these categories coincide with the belief issues outlined in the previous chapter.

TRANSFORMING
PERCEPTIONS OF SEPARATION
INTO AFFIRMATIONS OF ONENESS

1.   SELF-WORTH

Feelings of Separation	Affirmations of Oneness
I feel unloved.	I am open to love. I am worthy of love.
I give much more than I receive.	As I give, I receive the unlimited loving energy of the universe.
I feel like I am a bad person.	I choose to be compassionate and forgiving with myself and others.
I don't deserve to experience happiness.	I am worthy of all of life's blessings.
I don't have the time to take care of myself.	I choose to create the time and space to nurture and regenerate myself.

2.   SELF-RESPONSIBILITY

Feelings of Separation	Affirmations of Oneness
I have no control over what happens to me.	I take responsibility for the perceptions I choose and how they affect my life.
I cannot survive without someone to take care of me.	I am connected to a Higher Power that provides me with the strength and courage I need to support myself.

My parents have ruined my life.	I am responsible for the quality of my own life.
Bad things are always happening to me.	I choose to see the spiritual messages in all of my experiences.
People are always trying to control me.	I have the power to take charge of my own life.

3.   ATTITUDE

Feelings of Separation	Affirmations of Oneness
Life is an endless struggle.	I choose to see life as a process of learning and growing.
It will never work.	I am open to success and positive outcomes.
The world is a rotten place.	I choose to see divine will and goodness in all things.
I have to fight to get what I want.	I choose to experience peace and harmony in my life.
I can't do it.	I choose to believe that anything is possible.

4.   INNER-POWER

Feelings of Separation	Affirmations of Oneness
Life's a game—I've got to stay on top.	I choose to treat myself and others with kindness and respect.

I am telling you this for your own good.	I choose to help others by being a compassionate listener and setting a good example with my own life.
I'll tell you what's wrong with you . . .	I am open to seeing the spiritual goodness in all people.
I want you to change_____ _____.	I am aware that the only person I have the power to change is myself.
You should _____.	I choose to release all judgment and criticism of myself and others.

5.   COMMITMENT

Feelings of Separation	Affirmations of Oneness
I don't even know who I am.	I am an expression of universal light and love.
I don't know how to express myself.	I am spiritually guided to express my true self.
I am afraid to express my real feelings.	I am willing to express my genuine self.
My creativity is blocked.	I am an open channel for receiving and expressing my divine creative energy.
I am afraid I will fail.	I am completely supported by the universe when I express my truth.

6. OPENNESS TO CHANGE

Feelings of Separation	Affirmations of Oneness
I am afraid to change.	I am safe as I flow with the creative, loving energy of the universe.
How do I know what choices are "right" for me?	I am guided by universal wisdom to make choices in my greatest good.
What if I make the "wrong" choice?	I now see that every choice I make contributes to my growth and wholeness.
I'll wait until tomorrow.	I choose to be in the present.
I'll wait and let fate decide.	I am aware of my inner power to choose perceptions that are aligned with Divine will.

7. TRUST IN THE UNIVERSE

Feelings of Separation	Affirmations of Oneness
There is no reality beyond this physical world.	I am open to perceiving universal truth.
I am afraid to trust and let go.	As I let go, I open myself to receiving love.
I feel lonely.	I am open to experiencing a connection with a higher spiritual reality.
I can't depend on anybody.	I open myself to the benevolent abundance and support of the universe.
How can I believe in something I can't see or touch?	I am open to expanding my perceptions.

These are only a few examples of affirmations. Transforming our thoughts is certainly not a process which is confined to this exercise. Each one of us has the ability to take absolutely any negative self-thought and immediately turn it around into a constructive, positive thought every moment of every day.

We can retrain our minds by catching ourselves when we are saying something negative or unkind and immediately reframing our thoughts into a more positive message. By imagining our minds as a tape recorder, we can rewind and tape over. When we are aware that we are thinking an unkind thought, such as, "I never succeed at anything," stop immediately and change the message. Do a mental rewind and tape over a more loving message, such as "I deserve success."

Affirmations help us to develop the habit of consistent, positive self-dialogue. Simply being conscious of how we think and talk has very powerful effects because it offers us the ability to consciously choose what we want to store in our subconscious minds. Our internal dialogue creates the subconscious reservoir of all the beliefs which fuel how we feel about life. We need to take extraordinary care to feed it with thoughts of kindness and love because what we put into it is what feeds back to us.

Part Three

Awakening to Oneness

Chapter Eight

Creating Visions of
Our Desired Reality

Throughout these pages we have been working on our personal healing in order to coincide our personal perceptions with our spiritual truth of Oneness, starting with unconditional love of self. The more we evolve in our personal spiritual healing, the more apparent it is that there is a large gap between our present physical reality and the ideal experience of a world of unity and wholeness. How, then, do we get from where we are to where we want to be? How do we stretch out into new realities which we have never seen with our physical eyes?

We all have dreams tucked away in our minds of our ideal version of life. Whether we remember or not, each of us has the awesome ability to bring our dreams of a kinder, more enlightened world into our reality through the practice of creating visions. *Visions* are mental pictures, inspired by the soul, clarifying what we want to experience in our lives. Webster defines a vision more formally as *something seen otherwise than by ordinary sight; a vivid picture created by the imagination*. While ordinary sight is our ability to see tangible things with our physical eyes, we also have the extraordinary capacity to see from an infinitely, more expansive perspective—we can see with our mind's eye (also known as our "third eye") by imagining something we want to see which is not yet visible in our concrete physical world.

What Is the Purpose of Creating Visions?

Visions give meaning and purpose to our lives because they are the mental images which guide our actions toward a desired outcome. When we truly understand this, it is hard to imagine why we would ever want to live our lives without conscious visions. Most of us would not consider building a house without a blueprint of how we want it to look when we are finished—we wouldn't mindlessly start digging out foundations, drilling holes, and nailing up walls without any idea of what we want to create. Yet when it comes to the most important structure we can ever build, the context of our lives, we tend to aimlessly react to situations without ever taking the time to envision the ideal of what we want to accomplish.

How Do We Know What We Want to Envision?

The seeds of our visions are within our dreams. How many times have we heard ourselves and others say, "I feel so flat," "I don't even know who I am," and "I don't know where I am going with my life?" When we say these things, it sounds as though we are waiting for someone else to assign us a dream so we can be inspired.

Of course, we are each responsible for our own dreams and what we do with them. The value of dreams cannot be overestimated because they are truly the sparks of light within our spiritual core that fuel our passion for living. Without our dreams, it feels like life has no purpose. Yet in order for dreams to come true, we must first know what they are.

When we speak of dreams, most of us think of the unconscious messages we receive as we sleep. Our nighttime dreams link our conscious with our subconscious and reveal our innermost thoughts and feelings. Night dreams typically speak to us in metaphors and symbols. Although they many times appear to make no sense (from a logical point of view), they often provide us with spiritual guidance and insight.

Our dreams are not only revealed in the unconscious messages received as we sleep but also in the conscious desires we carry within our hearts, begging to be expressed in our actions. How do we know what our daydreams are? Our daydreams express our aspirations and are many times revealed in the "I've always wanted to" statements we find ourselves saying; that irrepressible inner drive we have to do something no matter how illogical it may seem; and the inner voice that relentlessly speaks to us of things we need to do in order to honor our need to genuinely express our true self.

Every one of us is internally programmed with special and unique talents to contribute to this world. The memory of our individual spiritual gifts, as well as the potential to manifest them, is seated within our dreams. If we have suppressed our heartfelt desires for a long time, we may think we no longer have any dreams. The truth is that no matter how long we have squelched our dreams of what we want to achieve in our lives, they remain within our hearts until we claim them.

All too often we take our unexpressed dreams to our death, so one way to bring our dreams to conscious awareness is to imagine that we are present at our own funeral listening to our eulogy. What would we like to be said of our accomplishments during our time on earth? Perhaps we want to be remembered as a dedicated parent, an aficionado of fine arts, a healer, an entrepreneur, or a tireless crusader for humanitarian causes. Whatever we want to be remembered for—these are the things we need to be working on in the present.

It is our purpose in life to awaken to our dreams by exercising our human inner power to bring them into our physical reality through the power of visions.

How Can Visions Make Our Dreams Come True?

Visions make it possible for our dreams to come true by transforming the passive mode of merely wishing for something into the far more dynamic, self-empowering state of seeing it in our minds as though it already exists. A vision is a guiding light magnetizing us toward a desired outcome.

Some people sense their inner power to envision their dreams into existence very early in their lives. They are the charismatic personalities indelibly ingrained in our memories, such as Michelangelo, Albert Einstein, Eleanor Roosevelt, John F. Kennedy, and Martin Luther King. Their visions have served as beacons of light magnetizing the energies of large numbers of people to stretch toward a larger, more magnificent picture of humanity. While these people are paragons of our human capacity to create changes through visions, we don't have to be world-renowned to have personal visions that affect the entire world. Every single human being, no matter what our station in life, has the ability to consciously create visions which improve the quality of our personal lives and, therefore, the lives of all others.

While dreams are the seeds of all new possibilities, desires are only a beginning. Dreams can only come true if we support them with our actions, and, as always, our actions are a choice. We can smother our dream sparks by ignoring our heartfelt desires and continuing to live within a whirlpool of stagnant ideas that are never acted upon. When we do this, we get locked into the perpetual "if only" state of being where our physical reality never quite seems to be in synch with what we really want. When we choose to consistently ignore our inner sparks, it becomes increasingly difficult to remember our dreams, and we eventually feel that we are merely surviving rather than living. Perhaps this is what Henry David Thoreau innately understood when he wrote, "The mass of men lead lives of quiet desperation."

We can also *ignite* our dream sparks by planting the seeds of our dreams into visions which inspire us to expand toward greater, more enlightened spaces. We can invariably pick up on the energy of people who ignite their dreams— they are the ones who are vibrant and enthusiastic with an energy that feels electric. They walk like they know where they are going, and their mere presence can lift the energy of an entire room. These are the people who seem to know how to plug their dreams into the powerhouse of universal energy, demonstrating that "hitching our dreams to a star" is far more than a myth.

The time is *now* to awaken to our inner power to activate our dreams! The first step in realizing our dreams is to proclaim in very clear terms what it is we want to see within our lives. We do this through the process of creating vision statements clarifying what we want to see.

How Do We Create Powerful, Energizing Vision Statements?

Like affirmations, there are certain essential factors which enable us to consciously coincide the energy of visions with spiritual principles, thereby raising their vibration. The higher the vibration, the more quickly visions can actualize. Following are some very important components for formulating powerful vision statements:

Stated In The Positive—Our society is in the habit of concentrating on problems. Visions concentrate on resolutions. This is an extremely important point because the energy of creative resolution is much more powerful than the energy of focusing on problems. When we are focusing on the positive, we are using our energy to create and we feel empowered; when we are focusing on the negative, we are using our energy to react and fall victim to fear. Visions of fear do not support our human potential to grow, so they do not resonate at a very high frequency.

Positive statements create positive results and perpetuate an expansive energy. Notice the difference between how we feel when we make a statement in the negative, "I see that I am not sick, tired, or weak anymore" compared with a positive version of the same statement, "I see myself as an active expression of vibrant health and spiritual strength." The first one has the feeling of hiding in a shell, the second one of bursting with life and energy!

Seen As Already in Existence—It is essential to begin with proactive words in present tense, such as "I see" when we write and verbalize vision statements. The words "I wish" and "I

want" are passive and imply that we are waiting for something
to happen to us rather than claiming our responsibility to utilize
our energies in harmony with the universe to create what we
want. When we say "I wish," "I want," and "I desire," we are
creating a reality that totally complies with these words. Rather
than actually receiving the blessings of our visions, we produce a
perpetual state of wanting and wishing for them.

Visions declare the specific reality of something we want to
see as though it is already in existence. This opens up the space
for universal circumstances to support what we want to see in
our lives. As the popular quote from the movie, "Field of
Dreams," puts it, "Build it and they will come."

Perhaps one of the best examples of this is the Declaration
of Independence, part of which reads:

"We hold these truths to be self-evident, that all men
are created equal, that they are endowed by their
Creator with certain unalienable Rights, that among
these are Life, Liberty, and the pursuit of Happiness."

This was quite a remarkable declaration, considering it
was signed on July 4, 1776 in present tense, as though it were
a *fait accompli* when, in fact, the actual Peace Treaty for the
Revolutionary War was not signed until seven years later on
September 3, 1783. The Declaration of Independence was not
a result of the United States gaining its freedom, it was the
cause of it. In essence, it was a collective vision inspired by the
unified heart of the American people which opened the space
for a whole new reality.

Include Self—We each author our own expression of
inner truth, so we are personally accountable for honoring
our dream sparks. Accordingly, our vision statements need to
begin with "I" as we acknowledge the spiritual truth that all
change begins within self.

Although our vision statements need to include self, it is
very powerful to envision that the same blessings which
improve our lives also bless the lives of others who are open
to receiving them. For example, "I now see that my life
attracts and reflects positive energy" can be made even more

powerful by adding "I also see that my positive attitude and joyful life have a positive effect on everyone around me who is open to this blessing." Although all changes begin from within, the ripple effect of our own healing touches everything and everyone around us—especially when we see it as so.

Expressive of Our True Intention—Again, we need to be aware of the power of our words by taking responsibility to say what we really mean. A young woman who attended one of my vision workshops called her mother, a friend of mine, to relate a humorous story which attests to this.

My friend said her daughter, Jessica, had broken off a dating relationship with a man named Rob. Jessica felt uncomfortable with the angry overtones to their separation and desperately wanted to see Rob once more to bring their relationship to peaceful closure. She decided to try out the power of visions, in what she perceived as a small way, by offering the following simple vision statement to the universe: "I now see that Rob and I meet at a social engagement and that we have a very easy and friendly conversation." As her mother related this story to me, she was giggling the entire time.

"Why are you laughing?" I asked her.

"Because Jessica went to three parties last night and met a man named Rob at every one of them. She says she never got a chance to talk to anyone other than the three Robs, none of whom was her former boyfriend!"

This story shows that we need to be clear of what our true intention is and to express that specifically in our vision.

Incite Positive Emotions—Visions are of the spirit, and our spirit comes through the emotions of the heart. When we put the excitement of our true feelings in a vision we create momentum. For example, we can have a vision statement that says, "I see myself in a job I really like," but it doesn't incite nearly as much enthusiasm and interior motivation as, "I see myself in a career in which I vibrantly express my spiritual purpose as I experience abundance, joy, peace, and harmony."

There is something very magnetic and powerful about a vision based on a passionate desire for good. If Martin Luther King had made an unemotional speech advising us that it would be a good idea to embrace diversification in humanity, it is questionable whether most people would have remembered his message. Instead, he made an impassioned plea in his "I Have A Dream" speech in which he implored people to join him in envisioning the unity of all humanity as a reality. It was his inner fire that caused the message of unity to resonate at a very deep level within so many people and to remain alive to this day.

A Stretch Beyond Our Present Status—The magic of visions is that they stimulate us to stretch toward greater possibilities. While visions do actualize, we are never finished with them because we can always expand our world by creating larger, more dynamic visions which move us closer to Oneness. If we make our visions too small or too vague, we are not creating the constructive tension that is necessary to snap us into a new reality. In fact, many times our visions have already come into being, and we forget to create broader new ones.

During one of our workshops, Claire, a lovely woman who provides child care for children of working parents, said she was using the same vision for a long time but was not experiencing any results. She offered the following as a statement of her vision, "I see that I have a career which has great significance." It was interesting that almost everyone who heard her vision statement was surprised that she did not recognize that she was already in a career of tremendous significance, not only to the parents of the children, but to all of society.

I asked her, "Is there something that you really want that goes beyond what you have expressed in this vision?"

"Well yes," she said shyly, "actually I would like to earn more money and open myself to some new opportunities, but I thought it might be too big a stretch to say that." With encouragement, Claire expanded her vision statement to "I now see that the universe provides me with the perfect opportunities to joyfully share my spiritual gifts as I am abundantly rewarded in all ways that are in my greatest good." She said she had felt bland when she shared the first vision and that this one made her feel like she sparkled. We could all see that she did!

Open To All Possibilities—This is an extremely important point which is frequently overlooked. While a vision statement can be specific about our imagining a positive outcome and the way we want to feel,

IT IS IN OUR GREATEST GOOD TO RELEASE THE SPECIFIC WAY IN WHICH THIS HAPPENS, AS WELL AS WHEN IT HAPPENS, TO THE UNCONDITIONAL LOVE OF THE UNIVERSE.

A pragmatic example of this would be a vision statement for a car. If we state, "I see myself getting a brand new red BMW by January of next year," this may come true; however, it may or may not be the best car, color, or time for us to get it. We may love the car and find that it is much more expensive than we want to pay or we may get the car under very unhappy circumstances. On the other hand, we can put our desires for a car into a much more effective vision statement by saying something like, "I see that the universe provides the perfect car for me at exactly the right time in my life. This car is affordable and brings great joy into my life, as well as the lives of everyone involved."

I used these statements when I was looking for a car. Within two days of my vision a friend phoned to tell me about a car her neighbor was selling. I called her neighbor—the car was exactly what I wanted and in perfect condition, but it had just been sold. I humored myself by thinking it was probably not the right car anyway because it was $600 more than I wanted to spend. The following day I left town for a two-week vacation. Upon returning, there was a message on my answering machine saying the person who had wanted to buy the car had changed his mind—did I still want it? I accepted the offer and had a delightful surprise when I went to withdraw money from my mutual fund to pay for the car—the stock market had gone up within those two weeks, and I discovered that my investment had appreciated by exactly $600! The gentleman selling the car was equally pleased because his new car had arrived two weeks later than he had anticipated.

When our vision statements leave space for universal resolution, we put our dream sparks into the gap which bridges our physical reality with the infinite potential of spirit. This catapults our desires into a space of all possibilities. When we perceive the universe as the energy of unconditional love, we begin to see that no matter how large or small our visions are, they manifest in ways that far exceed what we can humanly imagine because they are answered in ways that are for the good of the whole.

What Are Some Examples of Dynamic Vision Statements?

In summary, in order to use our personal energy in harmony with the universe, vision statements need to be:

- Positive
- Present Tense
- Personal
- Precise Intention
- Potential–Infinite
- Passionate

While including all these factors in a vision statement may seem overwhelming at first, it is truly quite simple and very natural. No matter what form we choose to clarify and remember our visions, it is essential that we reinforce them through both written and oral statements. This simple act allows us to proclaim entitlement to our dreams which are in our greatest good in an immediate and practical way. Following are some examples of vision statements which employ these dynamic factors:

Health:

- I now see that I am healing at all levels of my being in ways that are in perfect accord with divine will.

- I see that I am whole—body, mind, and soul.

- I see my body, mind, and spirit resonating with the radiant light and endless love of the universe as I heal at all levels of my being.

Abundance:

- I see myself as an open, active channel effortlessly receiving and sharing universal abundance which comes in all forms and all ways that bless me and everyone around me.

- I see myself joyfully and effortlessly receiving and sharing abundance in all forms and in all ways that are in my greatest good and the greatest good of all humanity.

- I see an endless supply of universal abundance flowing to and through me in the perfect forms, in the perfect ways, at the perfect times.

Relationships:

- I see myself constantly expanding in my capacity to receive and express unconditional love.

- I see that I am increasingly treating myself with love and respect, and that I attract people who love and respect me in all of my relationships.

- I see light and divine purpose within myself and within everyone whom I meet.

Work:

- I see myself in a career which is in perfect accord with my spiritual purpose, abundantly rewarded and surrounded with people who appreciate me, as I joyfully express my inner truth through my work.

- I see myself as a willing, active expression of divine love in all that I do.

- I see myself in a career in which I vibrantly express my spiritual purpose as I experience abundance, joy, and peace within myself and with others.

Are Vision Statements the Same Thing As Affirmations?

There are similarities in the energy of vision statements and affirmations in that they are positive, about self, and in the present tense. The difference is that affirmations are the words we choose to *transform* our personal basic beliefs of separation into positive ones that are based on the spiritual truth of Oneness. Visions are mental pictures of how we want to *manifest* these beliefs into new possibilities that enhance the quality of our lives. In other words, positive affirmations form the foundation of beliefs that supports our ability to create and manifest visions which create greater, new realities. For example, a vision statement for a person with a food addiction might be, "I see my body at the perfect weight, working in harmony with spirit, as I experience perfect health, joy, and inner peace." A supporting affirmation to reinforce the basic belief of self-worth necessary to achieve that vision could be, "I love and accept myself and am motivated to choose foods and eating habits that support my health."

What Are Some Ways in Which We Can Reinforce Our Visions?

Visions are most powerful when they feel so real we can almost "taste" them as we anticipate their actualizing into physical form. This anticipation reinforces our trust in the universe to bring our mental pictures into reality. The ways in which we do this depend on our personalities and nature.

Here are a few suggestions:

Written and Verbal Statements—Words have creative power! At the very least, it is extremely important to confirm the essence of our visions with written and verbal vision statements. This is essential because we are immediately affirming our new mental images in a form which allows us to verbalize them repeatedly to ourselves and with supportive others. **Like affirmations, we need to repeat vision statements to ourselves and supportive others until we totally believe in them.**

Pictures and Drawings—Visions can be literal or metaphoric. Pictures depicting our visions can be cut out of a book or magazine or hand drawn. Drawing pictures of them provides a very holistic and composite perspective which stimulates our imagination. It does not matter if we draw stick figures or elaborate, detailed pictures, so don't worry about your artistic skills. All that matters is that the pictures trigger the memories of our visions and that we look at them frequently.

Conversation—This includes internal self-dialoguing as well as conversations with others. Talking about our visions with supportive people is great fun and extremely beneficial. Hearing ourselves talk about things we really want to see in our lives generates a positive spirit and makes our ideas feel real. It is important to do this with people who affirm our true nature and commitment to spiritual growth. This is a contagious process because positive people have a natural desire to participate in energizing conversations.

Journal Keeping—When we keep a journal of our visions and our dreams, we have the benefit of seeing how they come true and how we keep expanding. We can also see patterns in areas of our lives that are beckoning to be healed.

Physical Enactment—Acting out our visions as we think about them, such as dancing or walking, is very effective because it integrates our thoughts into action. This can also be done in the form of acting as though the vision has already been realized. For example, if we have envisioned a new house, it is very significant to begin looking at houses as though we already have the money and the perfect house is waiting for us. When we do this, we are sending a message out to the universe that we trust our visions are in the process of manifesting.

Meditation/Visualization—It is very powerful to hold the images and, in particular, the feelings of our desires in the subconscious level of our minds during a quiet, meditative state. It is within this space, when we are free from outer distractions, that we feel our true inner connection with universal intelligence.

What Are Some Suggestions for Incorporating Vision Statements Into Meditation/Visualizations?

Visions are predominantly a right-brain function because they are seen first with our imagination. Although we can create visions in a fully conscious state, we can increase our right-brain reception ability when we are in a deeper state of relaxation. We can do this in many ways, such as: focusing on our breath, listening to soft music, taking a walk, meditating, listening to a guided visualization, sitting quietly with nature, painting, or drawing.

Once relaxed, we need to give ourselves permission to dream—to be free to imagine anything we want. Then imagine the ideal picture of your vision statements as though already accomplished. For example, if your vision is about health, perhaps you might see light pouring into the top of your head and radiating into every molecule of your body as you see yourself pulsing and glowing with good health. If you are imagining forgiveness, you might see yourself shaking the hand of someone or your heart expanding with light. The important thing is to remain open and accepting of whatever comes to your mind without any judgment, whether it be pictures, words, colors, symbols, music, or anything else.

Pay attention to the details of what you are seeing with your imagination and absorb them with all of your senses—

feelings, colors, temperature, brightness, tastes, and smells. All of these senses activate different neurons in our brains, allowing us to perceive our mental pictures as physical reality. Allow yourself to enhance your mental picture according to your intuition; such as, adding more color or bright light. If you are someone who does not typically see graphically, it is just as effective to make note of your thoughts. When you are ready, write down what you saw or thought and/or draw a picture of it so as to bring it into physical form.

What About Those of Us Who Do Not See Mental Pictures?

This question comes up many times because most of us have been socially indoctrinated to use our pragmatic left-brain logic to handle the majority of our situations. Even though it may feel foreign to call upon the imaginative powers of our right-brain, it is a process which is an innate part of our human nature and available to everyone.

Every person thinks; therefore each of us is in a perpetual state of creation. Because we are all unique, the way in which ideas come to us depends on our sensory perception. If we imagine only words, it is every bit as powerful as pictures because we are still using conscious intention to manifest our thoughts. The key is to relax and allow our visions to come to us in any form that is natural. With practice, we can become more comfortable with mental imaging because we increasingly learn to trust the process as we witness how our visions expand our energy.

How Do Visions Expand Our Energy?

Visions expand our energy because they reach out beyond the confining boundaries of an existing situation. Visions do not deal merely with what we are seeing with our physical eyes; rather, they focus on much larger pictures in which we imagine greater possibilities than we are presently experiencing. When we do this, we no longer act like a puppet being controlled by the world as we wait for things to change; instead, we can be an active participant making things happen by utilizing visions as energetic tools to work in concert with the universe.

The key word here is conscious—we can expand our energy by deliberately creating mental pictures which portray something in accordance with what we want to create. The positive effect on our energy is immediate, as experienced by David, a bright, young salesman who asked if we could get together to discuss his breathing difficulties and "impossible" work situation.

David had recently completed an extensive three-month sales training program. While he had enjoyed this course, he felt as if he had hit a brick wall when he finished his training and started as a novice salesman making numerous daily "cold calls" on prospects. He was in his third week of actually being on the job and was feeling very discouraged and deflated. David said he felt as if there were a clamp on his chest constricting his ability to breathe.

After asking him several questions, we both came to realize that David, like most of us, was not aware of his inner power to create visions. I suggested to David that he was in a position with enormous freedom and that perhaps he was looking to be defined rather than using his new position as a vehicle to help him create what he wanted. I invited him to consider the possibility that he may be feeling trapped because he had no mental picture of what he wanted to create through his job.

We started to work together on the visions process outlined in this chapter. As David began to see his job as a path to a vision, rather than a destination within itself, he saw many new opportunities to apply his talents toward realizing his dream. Within only five minutes David's chest began to relax, and he was able to take deep breaths with total ease simply by diverting his energy from worrying to envisioning the potential he saw within his reach.

Work is just one area in which we can employ visions—we can envision a new reality in absolutely any area of our lives. Envisioning the mind and body as healthy and strong, even when we are in a state of disease and illness, can have tremendous positive impact on our physical well-being. In fact, medical practices are increasingly integrating the process of creative visualization as a vital part of overall healing programs for people suffering from serious and chronic illnesses.

Visions can be as expansive as we want them to be, as long as we include ourselves within them. We can envision peace within as well as world-wide peace; more prosperity within our lives and the lives of everyone around us; more loving personal relationships and a world of unconditional love; and mental, emotional, and physical health within our personal lives as well as the health of the entire earth. This is what makes visions so exciting—we can apply them to absolutely every situation because visions tap into our inherent ability to utilize our energy in concert with our higher spiritual power to expand our reality! Our visions always expand our potential, but we have to be completely open as to the way in which this happens.

What Is Meant by "Remaining Open?"

We tend to have fixed ideas on how our visions will manifest; and yet, as we have already discussed, their very power lies in releasing the outcome to the infinite potential of the universe. Many times our visions actualize in ways that are completely surprising to us. This is because they frequently do not manifest in ways that fit our paradigms of what we are expecting to happen.

Let's take a look at the visions of David, whom we just met, and Harriet—two people who created visions regarding their careers. Their intention was the same—to expand their career potential—yet the outcomes were entirely different.

David called me two weeks following our meeting to tell me that his situation at work had rapidly improved after our session. He said that he was getting up in the morning actually looking forward to going to the office. David said he had decided to share his visions and goals with his sales manager and was surprised at how pleased his manager was to see his change in motivation and new outlook. "Guess what?" he asked excitedly. "My boss offered me the opportunity to attend specialized courses which parallel my new goals and one of the really successful guys in the office offered to be my mentor!" (David also gained another valuable insight—when we are clear as to what we want to accomplish, it becomes more obvious to those around us as to what they can do to support us.)

For Harriet, a young woman who had attended one of my vision workshops, the outcome was an entirely different story. Harriet came to see me several months after the workshop to share some of the experiences that had grown out of the visions she had created that day. One of her vision statements was, "I now see myself in a job which utilizes my talents in the perfect way while bringing me great joy, peace, and abundance within my life." Following is Harriet's feedback:

"I have to tell you that for four weeks following your workshop, I experienced nothing but havoc at work. Although I had been unhappy with my job for a long time, something was different after this vision. Suddenly, everything seemed to go from bad to worse. I couldn't even pretend to like my job anymore. The feeling seemed to be mutual—after a month of enduring this pandemonium, I was asked to transfer to another department. At first I was devastated—I took it as a rejection, and then I remembered how we had talked about the changes that would occur as a result of a new vision and my need to stay open. The bottom line is that I have to tell you I am really happy with the job I have been transferred to. It is completely different from what I was doing. In fact, I never even knew this position existed within my company—it seemed to come out of nowhere! I feel so expanded! I am using a lot more of my talents now and experiencing a new level of fulfillment. I am also more peaceful because I don't have to work overtime anymore so my family life is much better. I just never realized my vision would change the whole context of my job!"

In both these instances, David and Harriet opened themselves to outcomes that transcended their usual paradigms. While their visions manifested in entirely different ways, they both expanded their realities through visions which expressed their inner truth, resulting in outcomes which accommodated their true needs and desires.

Are Visions Synonymous with Goals?

Goals serve a definite purpose within our individual lives and social structures; but we have progressed to a stage of our human evolution requiring us to jump beyond the limitations of goals and into the infinite potential of visions. Goals are created with our left-brain logical thinking and work within established mental boundaries, whereas visions are inspired by our right-brain imaginative thinking and break us out of paradigms by opening our mental channels to limitless new possibilities.

Although we tend to think of them as the same thing, there are some very important energetic differences between visions and goals. Understanding the following distinctions allows us to utilize our energy more effectively:

Visions: The large, holistic view
Goals: The day-to-day decisions and actions

Visions: Inspired by the heart
Goals: Established by the mind

Visions: Something we *have*—an innate part of who we are
Goals: Something we set—external reference points used to determine our progress

Visions: Set point is the ideal, and we then use a picture of the desired outcome to stretch our objectives and goals to reach for it
Goals: Set point is where we are now, and we plot to move from this point to a pre-set destination

Visions: Initiated from within individuals emphasizing
                    personal values
Goals: Personally created or externally assigned to
                    individuals emphasizing desired, measurable results

Visions: Continuous process which expands as people grow
Goals: Pre-designated fixed points

Visions: A pulsation that pulls people toward it
Goals: A point we push to get to

Visions: Stated as though they are already in existence
Goals: Describe a future target

Visions: Describe something possible but are open as
                    to how they physically manifest
Goals: Describe a predictable result and how to
                    arrive there

Visions generate internal motivation and energy because
they are created by the values and feelings which come from
the soul. Our inner power to use visions opens the door of our
human existence to more light, more love, and greater energy
because the spirit can see infinitely further than our minds.

Aren't Visions Unrealistic?

Visions, by their very nature, represent our ideals—it is what makes them so powerful. Our spiritual truth is that anything is possible and, therefore, what is realistic is merely a matter of perception.

When we start with a goal, we begin with a pre-established possibility which we deem realistic because our left-brain says it is logical. Our growth is contained within the confines of the goal because we establish all of our actions within this paradigm of reality. This is something that frequently occurs in business meetings when we focus on goals—we think we are brainstorming when, in actuality, we are merely rearranging old paradigms.

When we utilize the energy of visions, we allow the imaginative power of our right-brain to introduce a much broader version of reality. Our growth rapidly accelerates as we rise to meet an expanded version of what is realistic.

Our visions are where our heart and soul want to be. Goals support visions by providing the plan of action which is necessary to bring our visions into physical reality. I saw the difference in the dynamics of visions and goals dramatically demonstrated by Linda, a wise president of a mid-sized company.

Linda called together a meeting of the employees and announced that the company was in financial distress. She shared that senior management had set a number of goals to save money, which included a freeze on salaries for the next two years. Understandably, her announcement was met with great anger and resentment on the part of many employees. She said she was sorry but could see no other way to save the company. "Well we have some ideas," said a man in the audience, "but no one has asked us for any of them."

Rather than fight the gentleman's comment, Linda said she would investigate ways in which the employees could share in resolving the company's financial problems. She employed a group vision process, facilitated by a neutral outside consultant, which incorporated everyone's ideas. The anger of the employees rapidly transformed into enthusiasm

as they shifted their focus from the problems to creating powerful visions of resolutions. The result of the visions process
was that the employees raised their goals to a much higher
level than the ones suggested by senior management because
they were inspired by their new vision. The employees not
only received their scheduled raises, the company had a stel-
lar year with profits that far surpassed the budgeted figures set
by management.

Certainly, it would be naive to think that we can set
visions and then just sit around doing nothing as we wait for
them to actualize. Visions actually perpetuate more expansive
agendas which typically generate dynamic programs of action
to reach toward them. Clearly, goals were a necessary part of
the process employed to save this company; but the goals
became significantly more effective when they were elevated
to meet with the new reality perceived by the group through
their visions. Individually and collectively, they had redefined
their version of what "realistic" is.

Is It Really Possible to Create a Whole New Reality Through Visions?

The universe frequently responds to our visions by flood-
ing us with a whole new set of opportunities to expand and
improve our lives. When our visions are in alignment with our
spiritual greatest good, blocks that are obstructing our progress
seem to dissolve, no matter how discouraging our present situation may be. The following true story of my close friend,
Kate, is inspiring testimony to this phenomenon:

Two years ago, Kate was involved in an abusive relationship, supporting a young child, and struggling to make a living
in a part-time job she was not enjoying. Because she could not
afford to live on her own, she continued to live with her
boyfriend and was experiencing the agony of the day-to-day
erosion of her self-esteem, as well as enormous guilt about
how her situation was affecting her child. Kate was overwhelmed—she did not know where to begin: she felt she
could not move out on her own because she had no money,

and she was having difficulty finding a job that would pay her enough to live independently while still having the flexibility and freedom to spend time with her young child. Adding to her complications, she was frequently ill because of all the pressure to change her living situation.

We worked together to create visions of a new reality for Kate. In spite of the chaos all around her, she was brave enough to take fifteen minutes every morning to close her eyes and see herself as whole, attracting prosperity, and being totally supported in all of her efforts to recover. Kate worked on affirmations to renew her self-esteem and wrote her vision statements in a journal. I noticed that she quickly became very mindful of her words. She started calling me daily to tell me of her dreams and visions for a better life. In spite of what she was seeing with her physical eyes, her mind remained open to a much more hopeful reality.

For two months Kate diligently continued to take a small part of each morning to focus on her affirmations and visions, when she called me one day to share some encouraging news—a former co-worker had called to tell her about a job opening. The job was exactly the type of work Kate had done before except it was on a consulting basis, paid much more than her former job, and she would have flexible hours. Within a week, Kate was offered and accepted the job. She was thrilled because she knew this opportunity would pave the way for her independence. Kate called and asked if I knew of any apartments which were available and in the location of a townhouse which my husband and I had rented out. I promised to check around. Within three hours of our conversation I received a surprise phone call from our tenant asking if she could break her lease because of a transfer she had just been offered. She asked me if she could possibly stay for only two more months rather than the six remaining in the lease. I excitedly called my friend, Kate, to tell her the apartment would be available within two months. Although she really wanted the apartment, she told me that she could not wait for two months because she felt it was necessary to get out of her present living arrangement immediately.

The next day Kate was standing in line at the bank when she struck up a conversation with a friend who told her he was in a bind: he had bought a new home without selling his former home. He said he really wished he could find someone who could live in his former house for a couple of months and be available to show it to potential buyers. In return, he would only ask that the temporary tenant pay the electric and phone bills. He asked Kate if she knew of anyone. Needless to say, Kate accepted the offer and was able to move into her friend's townhouse immediately. Two months later she made a totally smooth transition into our townhouse within a few days of our tenant's departure.

Kate now completely believes in the magic of visions and affirmations. She continues to practice creating them, and her blessings continue to unfold. It has only been two short years since Kate created her first vision of the quality of life she truly wants to create. She regained her health, and her salary more than quadrupled! Her lifestyle has dramatically improved: she is living in a beautiful townhouse, has bought all new furniture, a new car, and even received a scholarship for her son to go to private school. Since regaining her self-esteem, she has also resumed her favorite passion—dancing.

Kate's story is dramatic evidence of the power of visions and how they manifest in extraordinary ways. It is also an example that no matter how bleak our circumstances may seem, we always have the inner power to create new realities.

How Can We Strengthen Our Commitment to Envisioning New Realities?

Staying in the present and keeping our minds focused on our inner power to create new realities is a discipline that takes consistent practice and commitment. It is more than worth continuous practice because the rewards are amazing and energizing. There are a number of things we can do to reinforce our commitment:

Create Some Time Each Day for Self-Renewal

It is crucial to our spiritual well-being that we create a sacred space of time each day for self-renewal. One suggestion is to prioritize at least ten minutes daily, preferably in the morning when we are refreshed, to energize ourselves by creating visions and positive affirmations to support them. When we do this, we are mentally programming ourselves to think in a positive, constructive, creative way.

If this seems like too much time, think about the enormous amount of time and energy we waste when we are spinning out of control because we are out of balance and laden with stress. **Our spirit is the center from which everything else evolves. Is there anything more worthy of our time than our spiritual regeneration?**

Most of us awaken to fears and doubts each day. It is a very effective catharsis to jot down any bothersome thoughts of fear which are weighing us down on the left side of a piece of paper as "I feel" statements. We can then transform the negative energy of each of these statements by writing positive, uplifting affirmations and vision statements on the right side of the paper. For example, "I feel afraid to make my business presentation today" can be transformed in a matter of seconds to, "I see myself confident and poised as I deliver a highly effective business presentation today."

When we make a habit of doing this, we can avoid the accumulation of negative thoughts which snowball into physical, mental, and emotional blocks, thus keeping our minds free and clear to receive and express our flow of creative energy. With practice, we no longer need to write these transformation statements down—we can train our minds to instantly transform our negative perceptions into positive visions.

Surround Ourselves with Supportive People

It is also important to surround ourselves with people who support our spiritual growth. Some people are committed to trying to maintain status quo in their lives, in which case they are likely to discourage someone else's growth. People who perceive change as threatening have a tendency to overtly or subtly sabotage the spiritual growth of another through judgment and criticism. It is important that we be accepting and non-judgmental of others even if they disagree with our values and points of view. At the same time, it is generally not in our best interests to spend a lot of time with those who slow down our momentum by attempting to distract us from our path of spiritual growth.

If we do not have many people in our circle of friends and family who support our change and growth, we can utilize the power of visions by seeing that we magnetize loving, positive people into our network of friends. Interestingly, this is something which seems to occur naturally as we become conscious of our spirituality because the energy of our thoughts attracts people on the same wavelength.

Organize a Visions Support Group

It is also very reinforcing, as well as inspiring, to organize a group of like-minded people to meet periodically to share visions and dreams, to acknowledge manifestations of visions, and to listen to each other at a heart level. Talking about our visions to caring listeners enables us to become confident about our inner power to create. When we proclaim our visions by stating them aloud to attentive and caring people, we can receive constructive feedback enabling us to empower our visions even more. For example, our vision statements may overlook some of the important basics, such as saying "I wish" instead of the infinitely more powerful statement, "I see," or we may be saying "next year" instead of "now." When we become attuned to these basics, we can help each other to become much more effective at creating and manifesting visions simply by listening.

I learned the value of this when I organized and participated in a visions support group which met once a week. Initially, it was our intention to create a group vision affirming abundance in our lives and, through feedback, observe and share whatever changes we saw that coincided with the vision. Our group learned very quickly the importance of accurately stating what we wanted when we collectively created a vision in which we stated we were "open to receiving universal abundance in all forms and at all levels."

When we regrouped the following week, we discovered that each of us was being inundated by a surplus of everything—whether we wanted it or not. We laughed as we listened to each other's feedback—excess overtime, a barrage of mail, hoards of geese in someone's yard—you name it, we had more than enough of everything! It quickly became apparent, by listening to each other, that we had not been specific enough in our language. We changed our vision statement to say that we were "open to receiving abundance in all forms that were in our greatest good." When we met the following week and shared stories, several people in the group stated that they were receiving an abundance of good things but felt overwhelmed and exhausted. Clearly, we were still missing an important ingredient. Through these experiences we refined our skills in crafting vision statements for abundance, some of which follow:

> "We see ourselves as clear, willing, and active channels, effortlessly receiving and sharing universal abundance in all forms and at all levels which are in our highest good, while remaining healthy, centered, and at peace within."

> "We joyfully recognize our blessings with loving hearts."

> "We accept the gift of abundance in our lives and use it harmoniously for our good and the good of others."

> "We see our perceptions expanding to accommodate increasing abundance as we release all limiting belief systems."

Each of us continued to repeat these vision statements, along with many others, for a year. The results were phenomenal! In fact, the blessings which flowed into the lives of each one of us surpassed our greatest expectations. We reminded each other, through encouragement, love, and support, of our inner potential to envision new realities.

What If Our Visions Don't Seem to Be Manifesting?

Sometimes we may have visions which don't appear to be actualizing, no matter how many times we see them in our minds and say them aloud. When we feel this happening, following are a few questions which may be helpful to ask ourselves, as well as some suggested affirmations to help us get back on track. Remember, we need to repeat affirmations until they become incorporated into our belief system.

Do I Need To Forgive Someone?

One of the greatest stumbling blocks in our growth toward a more enlightened state of being is holding onto ill will toward someone. This impedes our ability to receive blessings because we are blocking our ability to receive love by retaining too much negative energy. If this is the case, we need to ask our higher spiritual self to help us to release these feelings. We can also practice the forgiveness exercise in Chapter Five. Many times the simple intention to forgive presents all the opportunities to make it possible.

Supporting Affirmation: I open my heart and mind to forgive myself and others.

Are My Visions Manifesting in
Ways of Which I Am Unaware?

We need to become very observant. Most times our visions are manifesting in larger ways than we can fathom. For example, if we envisioned we are healed of a physical ailment, we may be noticing that unresolved old relationships are suddenly facing us everywhere we look, or that debts suddenly need to be repaid immediately, or we could be fired from a highly stressful job to which we have been holding. Although on a superficial level things may seem to be worse, it could be that these situations are the root cause of the illness coming to the surface for resolution for a true spiritual healing working from the inside-out.

Supporting Affirmation: I open myself to being aware of the infinite ways in which the unconditional love of the universe is manifesting blessings in my life.

Is There a Basic Belief System
Which Is Sabotaging My Vision?

Our foundation of beliefs needs to correlate with our visions. For example, if we envision ourselves as great writers but continue to hold onto the self-limiting basic belief that we are not good enough to express our true talents to the world, we may have short-circuited the vision from manifesting. Once we are aware of the basic belief which needs to be healed, we can use affirmations like the ones in Chapter Seven to transform our feelings of fear to affirmations of Oneness which support our visions.

Supporting Affirmation: My basic beliefs are now expanding to accommodate the visions of my soul.

Am I Expressing My Visions in
Statements Which Resonate at a High Frequency?

When we first start expressing our visions in written and verbal form, we many times overlook something which, while seemingly insignificant, can make a huge difference in vibrational level. It is important that our vision statements really do include all the factors we have been discussing in this chapter, specifically that they be stated in the positive, be in the present tense, include self, express true intention, incite positive emotions, promote growth, and be open to all possibilities.

Supporting Affirmation: I am at one and at peace as I am divinely guided to create visions which resonate with the energy of unconditional love and light.

Is What I Have Envisioned in the Greatest Good Of All?

Sometimes we need to go back and revisit what we have requested. If we have done our visions correctly, we have done them with the intention that they manifest in a way that is in the greatest good of ourselves and others. We need to trust in the love of the universe to give us what is correct for our spiritual growth.

Supporting Affirmation: I am open to receiving the flow of blessings in my life in ways that manifest for the good of all humanity.

Is It Time to Create More Expansive Visions and to Do Them More Frequently?

Many times we like to think of visions as the end, the answer, the ultimate result. Visions are life, and life is an ongoing process. If we feel flat, chances are it is time to plant the seeds of more expansive, even more dynamic visions and to do it more often. This particularly happens after a period of complacency or when we have completed a major phase of our lives, such as a mother who is feeling empty as she watches her last child leave the nest. Although one cycle has ended, a whole new phase opens up and it is very inspiring to plant the seeds for new visions of potential.

Supporting Affirmation: I am flexible and willing to open myself to new challenges and opportunities which support my spiritual growth.

Is It Possible to Create Visions in a Conscious State of Mind?

When we consistently practice creating and articulating visions, eventually we no longer experience them as day-dreams or as a process separate from our conscious level of existence. Rather, we come to realize that we have the inner power to perpetually and instantaneously create a different reality simply by continuously seeing people and situations in their greatest light. The following personal experience attests to this:

I was in a long line in the supermarket recently. I couldn't help but notice that the checker was in a bad mood, as indicated by her curt responses and total lack of eye contact with anyone. I could see that people were very annoyed by her manner. One by one, I observed how the anger snowballed as each person progressed through the line. Rather than brace myself to deal with her, it took only a moment to move my attention from her negative behavior to seeing her in a different light: I chose to see her as a hard-working person who was open to responding in a positive way to the first kind gesture extended to her. As my turn came and I approached her, I said, "I can see you are working very hard today."

She lifted her head, looked directly at me with tears brimming in her eyes, and quietly said, "I'll tell you, it's more than just being busy—my little girl died three years ago today, and I am having a really hard time functioning."

I leaned across the counter and hugged her. "Thank you for your kindness," she said. "I think I can be nice to people for the rest of the day now."

As I walked away I realized that in the few seconds it took to envision her in a different light, a healing had taken place and I felt thankful for the privilege of being in her line.

We all have moment-to-moment opportunities to transform situations by envisioning them with more love. When we steadfastly continue to focus on the light within people and situations, visions are far more than an occasional mental picture we create for ourselves—they are an ongoing projection of our true spiritual self seeing the spirit within all others.

Chapter Nine

Integration

We came to this magnificent earth to *experience* our true spiritual nature by using our creative energy to manifest unconditional love into physical form. As we consistently practice aligning the intention of our thoughts, words, and actions with conscious visions which focus on the divine light and love within ourselves and others, we become whole. As we each become whole within ourselves, we have the strength to be whole with each other, and we experience *integration*.

Integration is the merging of our physical world with the truth of divine consciousness. Spiritual truth is the integration of polarities, the perfect balance resulting from the fusion of all the opposite extremes which exist in our physical world of polarity. It is in this neutral space that we remember our personal truth is the same as universal truth: *All of creation is inextricably connected to a unified field of love which is so vast, so kind, so accepting, so generous, so responsive, and all-encompassing that it transcends human explanation!*

We are each the embodiment of divine love.

Accordingly, we need to do much more than simply wish for a more enlightened existence—It is our spiritual responsibility to manifest the qualities of Oneness into our physical world.

What Are the Qualities of Oneness?

The qualities of Oneness reflect the balanced attributes of spirit: *unconditional love, wholeness, abundance, harmony,* and *joy.* These qualities are not polarized—that is to say they have no opposites—because they are the integration of both our feminine and masculine (yin and yang) energies. When we collectively integrate the thoughts of our minds and the actions of our bodies to coincide with the values of spirit, our society can become a World of Oneness that reflects these qualities.

What Is the Experience of a World of Oneness?

A World of Oneness is a reality in which we experience the ideal—it is perfect balance and the integration of all opposites into neutral, absolute form. When we evolve to this point, we no longer need to vacillate between the conflicting positive and negative poles which have served to help us experience the many facets of our total nature, and opposite ends of the spectrum of life will fuse into pure spiritual truth. Within Oneness, we experience the integration of energy in our personal and collective realities as follows:

- Love and fear combine and become **unconditional love;**

- Health and sickness combine and become **wholeness;**

- Peace and hostility combine and become **harmony;**

- Wealth and poverty combine and become a steady flow of **abundance;** and

- Happiness and sadness combine and become **joy.**

Unconditional Love

The most powerful energy that exists is unconditional love, for it is the eternal life force governing all of creation. With universal love, *all* things are possible—including an integrated physical world in which we experience unconditional love, wholeness, harmony, abundance, and joy. In a World of Oneness, we expand our perceptions of love to move beyond the control and judgment which are inherent in conditional love. **We remember how important it is to love ourselves because we realize the foundation of all our basic beliefs about life is contingent on how we feel about ourselves.**

When we honor ourselves, we also respect all other people, as well as everything in our environment, because we know that everyone and everything is a unique expression of divine energy which is interconnected. We remember that no matter what our skin color, sex, religion, nationality, age, or station in life, we are all on a spiritual journey to experience our spirit in this realm of life. It is through our diversity that we help each other to grow and to develop a sense of self in relationship to others. No matter what our individual differences may be, we remember that we are all souls who are growing, not only with, but because of, each other. We release the need to judge each other because we recognize that we evolve in as many ways as there are people and that we grow at our own individual pace.

Wholeness

In a World of Oneness, we expand our perception of total health to mean far more than the absence of illness and disease. In its most complete sense, health means wholeness, holiness, Oneness. When we are whole, we are healthy on every level of our existence.

On a spiritual level, we become healthy by taking personal responsibility to heal from our inner emotional core rather than looking for external fixes. We heal our wounded spirit by choosing to forgive ourselves and others and by becoming aware of the self-sabotaging behavior patterns that stand in the way of our spiritual growth. As we commit to transforming our feelings of separation to affirming the truth of our Oneness, our inner spiritual center becomes the foundation for how we live. Committing to truth frees our minds to choose healthy perceptions of Oneness based on self-love and our connection with all of life.

On a mental level, we integrate our thinking by balancing logic and intuition. We no longer label ourselves as "left-brained" logical or "right-brained" creative because we remember that we are all capable of whole brain thinking. When we are in Oneness, we each have the miraculous ability to access universal wisdom with our right-brain and to bring it into concrete form with our left-brain simultaneously and instantaneously.

On a physical level, our bodies become visible, radiant manifestations of our inner and outer congruence and we experience complete health and vitality. Because it is our true nature to be healthy, healing is even more contagious than sickness. As we heal within ourselves, we have the strength and energy to reach out a hand to energize and uplift each other. By doing this, we work together to create a chain reaction to heal our planet.

In a World of Oneness, our "world brain," the summary of the thoughts of all of us, also integrates. As the left-brain-oriented scientific, technological, and business aspects of our society attune to our intuitive right-brain connection to universal intelligence, our knowledge expands to comprehend the whole of our existence. Rather than competing, we are guided by our spiritual wisdom to cooperate with each other to use our collective knowledge to heal our global diseases: war, poverty, hunger, destruction of precious wildlife, environmental pollution, crime, and racial discrimination.

Harmony

Peace begins with individuals and nations agreeing to end hostilities. On a personal level, we are moving toward peace within as we resolve our inner conflict by choosing thoughts, words, and actions that are in accord with our spiritual nature to love. As we do this, we are innately motivated to resolve conflicts in our relationships with others, which rapidly fuels the impetus for world peace. As we experience peace within ourselves and peace with each other, we move toward the even more expanded state of peace—harmony.

Harmony means *accord, consonance, concert*. In a World of Oneness, our personal inner peace attracts other conscious souls with the same intentions and we become part of an infinitely larger harmonious union. Harmony does not mean that we agree with everyone about everything—it means we combine our differences to work in concert with each other for the good of the whole. Because we all vibrate at different levels, we are, in a musical sense, each a different instrument expressing a special sound. We have been living in a cacophonous world because we have been listening to only our own individual sounds. As we evolve to a higher level of spirituality, we attune to each other and harmonize our individual tones into a melodious universal symphony playing one song.

Abundance

The word *abundance* means far more than just having enough money—it is derived from the Latin root word, *abundare*, meaning *overflowing, copious, bountiful*. Abundance comes in every imaginable form: knowledge, money, health, friends, opportunities, food, clothes. When we truly experience abundance, we have everything we need exactly when we need it. As we move toward a more enlightened reality, we discard old paradigms that perceive the universe as a warehouse with a limited inventory, perpetuating the notion that we have to take from each other to get what we want because there is not enough to go around. We also realize that our own experience of having plenty of everything does not subtract from someone else's.

In a World of Oneness, we no longer confuse abundance with accumulation because we remember that the universe is a boundless, limitless, eternal flow of energy in all forms and that there is more than enough of everything for everyone. The universe is neither holding out on us nor is it punishing us. When we set our intention for any form of abundance with kindness and love, our capacity to receive is restricted only by personal perceptions of our worthiness to accept blessings. The more we understand that we are the essence of love, the more we are open to receiving. We awaken to the realization that we have not asked for too much—we have asked for far too little because the loving nature of the universe is generous and bountiful and seeks to fill all voids. In a World of Oneness, we know at the deepest level of our being that anything we envision can be a physical reality if we have the faith to believe that it is possible and the commitment to align our actions with our visions.

Joy

Joy is the perpetual celebration of life! To be joyful is to sense an inner buoyancy allowing us to feel uplifted and light-hearted. When we are joyful, we literally feel wonderful—full of wonder and open to constant growth. It is an inner passion that spontaneously expresses itself through our laughter, tears, and songs. Joy transcends the emotion of happiness because happiness is a polarized emotion subject to change depending on conditions and situations; joy, on the other hand, is an unconditional, consistent inner awareness of how exciting it is to experience both the positive and negative aspects of this awesome creative process called life.

When we live in Oneness, we know at our deepest level that no matter what we are seeing and experiencing, no matter how challenging our situations may be, we are always loved in all ways by our Supreme Being and, therefore, it is safe to jubilantly express our true self in all that we think, say, and do. Best of all, we join hands in a global celebration of life because we are open to sharing our greatest gifts with each other—the authentic expressions of the people we were born to be.

If It Is Divine Will That We Experience the Qualities of Oneness, Why Are We Not Experiencing Them in Our Present Physical Existence?

Humanity's greatest gift is the free will to choose perceptions that determine the ways in which we experience our spiritual growth. We then get to see how our concepts of life manifest into our physical experiences. While it is divine will that we ultimately return to our natural state of Oneness, we each have the right to choose the paths we want to take. If we were unilaterally told what to think, say, and do, we would not be able to choose how we want to access divine guidance, what questions we want to ask, how we want to interpret the answers, and how we want to incorporate them into the experience of our lives. We are not robots mindlessly carrying out orders—we are thinking, creative beings with a smorgasbord of opportunities from which to choose. If we were given no choices as to how to express our creative nature, what would be the purpose for living in this physical realm?

Do We Really Have the Human Capability to Co-Create a Physical World Which Is Ideal?

Because we are created in the energy of unconditional love, it is divine will that we choose perceptions which generate a physical reality of unconditional love, wholeness, abundance, harmony, and joy. When we align our human thoughts for creation with divine will, we are co-creating—which is to say, we are praying.

Prayer is the bridge which links our visions to universal spirit. When our visions coincide with universal truth, absolutely everything and anything is possible because we are living in concert with the laws of nature.

Heaven is not a place outside of ourselves—it is the internal, blissful memory of our unity with All That Is. We came from perfection. As our minds reunite with this remembrance, we realize that not only are we capable of bringing heaven to earth through the power of prayer—this is our spiritual mission!

How Do We Find the Time and Space to Pray in This Busy Day and Age?

Some of us might believe that prayers must be said in a special place, such as a church, temple, or synagogue; or maybe we have reserved prayer for special occasions and holidays; or as a last-ditch effort when we are in a crisis and feeling that we are out of options; or perhaps we thought we needed an intermediary, such as a religious official or a spiritual guru, in order to connect with our higher spiritual self.

As we awaken to our truth, we are remembering that we all have a direct spiritual connection with the Divine and that prayer is much more than a religious exercise—it is a human experience! We don't have to be sanctified in any way because our ability to pray is as natural as breathing. As we perceive prayer in this light, we also realize that it is not necessary to be in a state of panic and misery to justify praying, nor do we have to wait until we have free time or are in a special place.

In fact, prayer is so much a part of our nature that we can pray in a church or in a sports stadium, alone or in a crowd, with our eyes open or closed, aloud or in silence. The energy of our loving thoughts has an immediate and positive impact on the people and situations on which we are focusing. As we become fully aware that every thought we have, every word we speak, and every act we commit is manifesting our reality, we recognize that **our lives are prayer in action**.

Is There a Certain Way to Pray?

When we pray we are seeking guidance from our higher self and, when done with kind intention, there really is no wrong way to pray. While no one of us has a franchise on the ultimate prayer, there are certain ways to pray which are much more effective than others. When we become adults, we do not communicate in the same ways as when we were little children. As we grow older, we develop a stronger sense of self, our vocabulary increases, and we become more adept at knowing how to express what we mean. Likewise, as we spiritually evolve and expand our perceptions, it is in our greatest good to mature in the way in which we pray.

Many of us are skeptical of prayer because we have defined it according to perceptions of fear which separate our minds and bodies from our spirit. Because of this, prayer is commonly perceived as an impractical action which is isolated from our everyday lives. In the past, many of us have been taught to pray in a begging manner as though we were guilty and unworthy. At times we may have even plea-bargained with our Supreme Being (if you heal my child, I will go to church every week) as though we had to make a deal in order to get what we needed. If we were taught not to love ourselves or that we are innately filled with sin, we probably prayed out of dread that we might be punished because we were not "good." These types of self-attacking prayers are rooted in old paradigms based on fear and separation. As we increasingly remember that we are incarnations of universal love and light, we realize that the challenging situations we experience in our physical world are not punishments but opportunities which offer us chances to gain greater insights and more expanded perspectives about life.

When we no longer make a separation between our physical existence and our spiritual connection, we free ourselves to pray in an infinitely more powerful way. We realize we do not need to feel shy, apologetic, or intimidated as though we are addressing an earth-like vengeful, egocentric personality. Nor do we need to wait to ask for only the "big stuff," as though each prayer request we make is depleting a pre-determined ration of heavenly favors to which we are entitled. Seeking help from our divine source of love is much the same as a child calling home for direction and reassurance. As a loving parent, we would not feel as though we were doing our child a big favor by being available to offer assistance—we would be pleased to guide him or her home.

How Do We Co-Create?

We allow ourselves to experience the qualities of Oneness by consciously and actively participating in the process of co-creation. One way to do this is through vision prayers. A vision prayer aligns our visions of a more enlightened physical reality with our higher spiritual self. Most importantly, a vision prayer is based on self-love. As we remember we are not only capable of manifesting love, health, abundance, harmony, and joy in our lives, but that these qualities are actually our true spiritual nature, we then open our spirit to receiving the blessings which, from a divine perspective, have always been available to us.

The essence of the immortal message of Jesus, as well as countless spiritual masters of many religions, has been echoed so many times, in so many ways, and in every language: "Ask, and it shall be given you; seek and ye shall find; knock and it shall be opened unto you." And yet, are we really listening to this message? Indeed, the only reason we receive so few answers to our prayers is that we ask for so little!

It is such an awesome and wonderful truth that we find it difficult to believe: WE CAN ASK FOR ANYTHING WE NEED. If we feel cloudy as to how our prayers are being answered, we can ask for clarity and conscious indications which will make us more aware; if we don't understand why we are experiencing something, we can ask for insight; if we need direction, we can ask for conscious universal signs to guide us; when we feel blocked with anger, resentment, hatred, jealousy, or any other negative energy, we can ask for the grace to forgive ourselves and others; when we are lonely, we can ask to feel the presence of love; when we are out of money, we can ask to be cleared for an increased flow of abundance; when we are sick, we can ask to be aware of the underlying message of the illness and to be guided to our greatest form of healing.

The only obstacles which impede our capacity to receive the unlimited blessings of the universe are our own self-limiting basic beliefs and our unresolved issues of forgiveness. This is why a large part of this book deals with the process of healing basic beliefs of separation and opening our hearts to forgiveness. We can, therefore, perpetually increase the power of our prayers by making a life-long ongoing commitment to continuously confirm our basic beliefs of Self-Worth, Self-Responsibility, Positive Attitude, Inner Power, Commitment, Openness to Change, and Trust in the Universe. As for forgiveness, from the divine perspective, we are always forgiven for any transgression, no matter how large or small, because we are always loved unconditionally; however, it is absolutely essential that we consistently forgive ourselves and others in order to remain clear to receive the flow of universal love.

A vision prayer incorporates the dynamics of the manifestation principles we have been remembering together throughout this book. While praying in this way is not an original concept, until recently, it was considered primarily a mystical teaching shared by only a select few. My personal knowledge of this highly effective prayer process is something which has evolved gradually and naturally within the course of my own spiritual growth. I am guided to share this process because as larger numbers of us awaken to our inner creative power, it is imperative that we rediscover our individual and collective potential to envision greater realities.

The next few pages summarize a process to help us connect our visions with universal spirit through prayer. Although I have used specific examples for each part of the prayer process, it is important to note that **this guide can be used to pray for any vision you choose to manifest.**

This vision prayer process includes the following steps:

1. Align our thoughts with our higher spiritual power
2. Express thankfulness
3. Envision a greater personal reality
4. Envision our personal healing extending to others
5. Surrender the outcome to the love of the universe
6. Expect positive outcomes
7. Release the prayer

If, at first, it feels strange to pray in such a confident manner, **be patient and keep practicing.** Ironically, we are so accustomed to praying for the strength and courage to endure life, that it is an adjustment to think in terms of praying to increase our capacity to *enjoy* life!

Because this mode of praying is based on the spiritual truth of our Oneness, it resonates at an extremely high frequency and has the potential to manifest rapidly. No matter how unusual it may seem at first, constantly praying in this way tends to be highly motivating because the results are frequently so amazing that it reinforces faith in our power to co-create. With practice, consciously manifesting our visions in this way becomes so natural that it feels like we are dancing with the universe!

CREATING VISION PRAYERS

1. ALIGN OUR THOUGHTS WITH OUR HIGHER SPIRITUAL POWER

    i.e. *"I AM at one with The Source of Light and Ultimate Expression of Universal Love. I AM an open, active channel receiving and expressing unconditional love."*

We instantly elevate our vibration by beginning our prayers with *I am*, the most powerful two words known to man because they are the essence of ultimate creative energy. When we begin in this way, we are acknowledging our direct and personal connection with the unified field of love and intelligence and our inner power to co-create. When we align the will of our minds and the actions of our bodies to coincide with divine will, we are exalting our minds and bodies to resonate with the infinitely higher vibrational level of spirit, which clears the path for rapid manifestation.

Our individual religious and personal beliefs may guide us to use a specific name for "The Source of Light and Ultimate Expression of Universal Love," such as God, Heavenly Father, Highest Light, Creator, Great Spirit, The Absolute, and The All That Is. The important thing is that we begin our prayers by proclaiming that we are at one with the highest, most powerful energy of love that we can possibly conceive.

2. EXPRESS THANKFULNESS

    i.e. *" I AM thankful for all that is.*

The resonance of gratitude also raises our vibration and increases our capacity to receive. We can most certainly express our thanks for specific things; however, when we are also thankful for everything that exists, we honor the divinity in every person we meet, every challenge we encounter, and every situation we experience, whether it has been pleasant or not. When we do this, we broaden our perceptions to accommodate an even greater flow of blessings because we recognize the blessings in all that we see and experience. We can have answers to prayers all around us, but they only become blessings when we recognize them.

3.   ENVISION A GREATER PERSONAL REALITY

> *i.e. "I see myself joyfully experiencing peace within,*
> *health at all levels of my being, and abundance in all*
> *forms that are in my greatest good."*
> *(Any vision can be stated at this part of the prayer.)*

We plug our visions into the universal field of unconditional love and infinite potential by declaring what we want to experience in our lives as though it is already in existence. We can see it with our mind's eye or declare it through words—what matters most is that we express what we truly want. Again, our vision statements are most powerful when they are about self, in present tense, stated in the positive, say what we honestly mean, stretch beyond where we are, and open to outcomes which are for the good of all.

Expressing what we want may seem strange because many of us have forgotten that we can affirm our desires with our higher spiritual self. Because spirit is unconditional love, it is divine intention that we experience love, wholeness, abundance, harmony, and joy in our lives. When we ask for various forms of these blessings, we are working in total accord with divine will.

Our Higher Power already knows that we desire these qualities in our lives even before we ask because they are characteristics of who we truly are—so why bother praying? The purpose of affirming what we want is that *we* become *conscious* of how we choose to express these qualities in our

lives. In other words, we are taking responsibility to pro-
actively participate in the co-creation process by leading with
our minds rather than just waiting around to see what happens in our physical reality. This is why it is not sufficient to
pray, "You already know what I want, so make it happen."
Yes, our Higher Power does know what we want—the question is, do *we* know what we want? And if we do not have any
idea of what we want to see in our lives, how will we recognize when we receive support from the universe to manifest it?

When we take responsibility to clarify what we want to
create within the context of our lives and affirm it with the
energy of our words, and actions, we are doing the homework
that is necessary to enable our dreams to actualize.

4. ENVISION OUR PERSONAL HEALING
    EXPANDING OUT TO OTHERS

> *i.e. "I see my personal healing contributing to a World of
> Unconditional Love, Harmony, Wholeness,
> Abundance, and Joy."*

Each one of us affects all of us. As we heal our own individual lives, we can honor our personal responsibility to contribute to a world in which we can all experience the qualities
of Oneness by expanding our personal visions to a larger
world view.

5.   SURRENDER THE OUTCOME TO THE LOVE OF THE UNIVERSE

i.e. "I surrender this vision to the unconditional love of the universe."

Between our physical reality and our visions of new possibilities is a space in which we need to surrender ourselves. I often think of this part of prayer as being analogous to the part of the trapeze act when the artist lets go of one trapeze swing to catch another. This is the critical interim when we are suspended in mid-air in a space of pure faith and anticipation.

When we *surrender*, we let go of our ego's need to control the outcome, and we place the masterminding of how our prayers are answered into the hands of universal intelligence. Letting go does not mean that we just sit around and wait for things to happen. We still have to continue to live our lives, face our challenges, and continue to work through our growth issues. Nor does it mean that we get to escape from our responsibilities. In fact, surrender requires an extraordinary degree of self-responsibility and commitment to self-growth because we are opening ourselves to new possibilities which are likely to create a whole new agenda of action on our part.

When we surrender a prayer to the love of the universe, we are acknowledging the infinite wisdom of our higher spirit to provide resolutions that far surpass our grandest human plans because they are answered in ways that are for the good of the whole. Surrender means that we take responsibility to choose perceptions and create visions that clarify what we want to experience within our lives, but we *release the how* it happens to the universe. This opens us up to far greater possibilities because we don't have to predetermine, from our human perspective, whether something is possible. For example, we may envision that we have a career that is in perfect accord with our spiritual gifts, but have no idea how that can happen. If we were to bank on our own ability to make it happen, we would have a thousand reasons why it couldn't, and therefore it would not come true. But when we surrender the outcome to the universe, *anything* is possible because the universe has no restrictions on the infinite number of ways in which a prayer can manifest into physical reality.

Surrendering also means we are willing to accept divine will even if we don't understand it because we are aware that many times we cannot see the greater, holistic picture from our limited human perspective. When it seems that our prayers are not being answered, it is usually because they are being manifested on a profound level that is affecting the lives of many. In time, the larger picture reveals itself when we are ready to understand it.

I experienced this when my only child was seriously ill and I prayed with all my heart for her healing. I knew that I had neither the power nor the right to impose my version of how my prayers would be answered. While I remained clear about this, it became very challenging to remain open and accepting of how the universe was responding because it seemed that nothing was happening.

For months I continued to envision that my daughter was healing in all ways that were in her highest spiritual good, as well as the greatest good of everyone concerned. I prayed that her soul be open to the enormous love that was there for her; I prayed that she, as well as my husband, myself, and all concerned, be open to the messages her illness brought to each of us; I asked that my eyes be opened to enable me to see the divine goodness in all that was happening; and I affirmed that I was open to receiving all the strength and courage I needed to remain in a space of love, truth, and faith. I vividly remember releasing my child to a higher form of love and being totally conscious that it was the deepest level of surrender I had ever imagined possible. While I was at peace with this realization on a spiritual level, on another, more physical level, my heart ached as I wondered why, in spite of all my prayers and visions, nothing seemed to be happening.

The universal response to my prayers began to gradually unfold as not only did my daughter become strong, radiant, and whole, so did at least twenty other people who called me to tell me about all the blessings that had come into their lives as a result of their saying prayers in support of her healing. I was amazed at the feedback I began to receive. People opened their hearts to share stories of how their attitudes toward their spouses became more loving, how they were feeling more appreciative of their children, and how their physical ailments were dramatically improving. As one gentle friend so aptly put it, "It seems that all the beautiful things I am seeing for your daughter's life are happening in my own." This true story of my courageous child's recovery demonstrates how our prayers are actualized in ways that far surpass our human understanding, and that we cannot do good for another without inviting blessings into our own lives.

6.   EXPECT POSITIVE OUTCOMES

> *i.e.* "I know *this prayer is being answered in ways that are for the greatest good of all.*"

This is the **faith** part of our prayer and the point at which our limiting belief systems many times start to creep in. We often second-guess the power of our human spirit to create with divine energy. In fact, if we are totally honest with ourselves, we realize that many times we are more afraid that our prayers will be answered than we are that they won't. We might doubt ourselves by asking questions, such as: "Do I deserve to have my dreams come true?" "Do I have the strength to carry out what I have asked for?" "Is it really okay for me to ask for all these things?"

We can only receive what we believe we can receive. If, for example, we send out a thought form to the universe requesting increased wealth, followed by another thought form that we do not believe it can happen, one thought cancels out the other. When we do this, we undermine our own ability to receive the blessings we have requested. This is a bit like planting a garden one day and digging up the seeds the next day because we are doubtful that the seeds are taking root.

Pure faith transcends believing—it is KNOWING that our prayers are always answered, even if we cannot see it with our physical eyes. When we expect positive outcomes, we are acknowledging that our prayer has been heard and is accomplished according to divine will. Interestingly, the word *expect* is derived from the Latin words *ex* (from) and *pector* (heart). It is the nature of the universe to work in concert with the desires of the heart.

7.   RELEASE THE PRAYER

   i.e. " Amen."

   This is the part of the prayer where the intention of our vision is instantly transmitted to our Higher Spiritual Power. It is somewhat like clicking the "send" icon on an e-mail and trusting it to arrive at its destination. Depending on our beliefs, we may also choose other words, such as, "And so it is," and "so be it."

Isn't It Best to Reserve Our Prayers for the Really Important Things?

   We can always pray for direction and help with anything we need, no matter how large or small. There is no reason to hold out until we are desperate—our divine guidance is available to us every moment of every day. I am constantly filled with wonder at how our prayers are answered, even the ones in which we seek help with small, practical problems, such as my quest for a particular wallpaper. Hopefully, my true "wallpaper story" will inspire others to pray for guidance in all things.

   I had my kitchen wallpapered five years ago. When we recently redecorated our home, I found that I needed some more of the same paper for the other side of the room. The problem was that I didn't know the name of the manufacturer, the pattern name, or the pattern number. I recall one of my friends chuckling at my optimism in believing I could locate the paper five years later. And so I said a prayer in which I asked that if it was in my greatest good to find this paper, I be guided to the perfect source at the perfect time and that the search would be smooth.

When I awakened the next morning, I could not get a particular home decorating outlet out of my mind. The store is about thirty minutes from my home, and I headed toward the store with the directional instinct of a bird headed south for the winter. The moment I walked in the door my eyes met with the eyes of a pleasant gray-haired woman. I held out my meager little wallpaper sample and said, "I realize I'm looking for a needle in a haystack, but do you know where I can find this paper?"

"You're very lucky," she said. "I have been in this business for sixteen years, and I happen to have a photographic memory about wallpaper." She instantly identified the pattern and the manufacturer. "It's been out of print for a couple of years, but I know where we can find it—follow me," she said with total conviction.

Off we went, across a huge warehouse floor stocked with thousands of books of wallpaper. She strode directly toward a particular shelf, moved her hand half-way down and over to the right, and pulled out a book that instantly fell open to the exact page containing my pattern. "Is this it?" she asked. Before I even had a chance to answer her, she continued, "We still have three of these rolls in storage—will tomorrow be okay?"

"Perfect," I answered.

What About Praying for Others?

Whenever we pray for ourselves, we are automatically impacting everyone else in a beneficial way because each one of us affects all of us. Yet, there are many times when we feel strongly drawn through compassion to pray for specific others. While praying for others is tremendously effective and essential, it is imperative that we remember that how, when, and even *if* someone *wants* to heal is purely a matter of personal choice. At different times in our lives, many of us have chosen to stay stuck in our emotional patterns, and this is an individual choice which we need to respect in others as well, whether we understand it or not. Although we want to see people we care about free of pain and suffering, challenging situations such as illnesses, personal losses, and financial difficulties bring crucial messages that are unique to each of us in our spiritual process of growth. No matter how much we want to "fix" other people's problems, we have neither the right nor the power to intervene in another's manner of healing by praying for the particular solutions that we want for them.

We can, however, always pray for other people that they be in their correct spiritual space and then surrender their well-being to whatever religious or personal concept of universal love coincides with our personal belief systems. While there are an infinite number of ways in which we can do this, following are just a few ideas of things we can request for others through prayer while remaining in our own correct space of non-judgment and unconditional love. Of course, it is in our greatest good to ask for these same blessings in our own lives.

Some of the blessings we can request for others are that they:

- Remember they are a manifestation of divine love;

- Be open to their highest forms of healing and that they recognize how these opportunities reveal themselves;

- Be open to receiving and expressing unconditional love;

- See their own beautiful light within;

- Forgive themselves and others;

- Have the strength, faith and courage to act upon their inner truth; and

- Embrace the divine messages of their illnesses and/or difficulties in a timely, gentle way.

We can also ask to be guided as to how we can be of greatest support to the people for whom we pray and then listen to and act upon our inner guidance. When we pray in this type of neutral, detached-from-the-outcome manner, we are empowering others to remember their true spiritual self by our focusing on their light within. What could be more loving and empowering?

Praying for the good of others has astounding power, especially when two or more ("where there are two or more gathered in my name") people unite in their intentions to send loving, healing energy toward someone. Recently a client and dear friend of mine, Denise, had to undergo surgery for the removal of a brain tumor. It was an emergency situation, and I enthusiastically responded to her husband's urgent phone call requesting that I join with him and some of their friends to pray for her while she was in surgery. Denise is a woman of great faith in the power of prayer and integrative healing, and I sensed she was open to all the love we could send her.

When I prayed for Denise at the scheduled hour of surgery, I felt engulfed by an enormous wave of energy. I remember thinking at the time that it felt like I had just accessed a Spiritual Internet by joining forces with many other souls who were praying for her in that exact moment. I envisioned love within and all around her and that the doctors, nurses, anesthesiologist, and everyone involved were open to the wisdom and energy of the universe guiding them to be in their correct space. I envisioned brilliant light everywhere and that the entire room was lifted up to divine will.

Denise made a remarkable recovery and was back at work within a month, in her words, "feeling more alive than ever."

She also had an inspiring story to share. She remembers a woman standing over her hospital bed just prior to her surgery simply saying, "I am here to pray for you."

Denise said, "I thought it was a cleaning person, but I am not sure—what I am sure of is that I felt an overwhelming sense of peace and love in the presence of this woman whom I had never seen before." After her surgery, the head surgeon told Denise that some-thing miraculous had happened which he had never before witnessed in all his years of experience. He said that when he made the incision, a tumor the size of a grape literally jumped out into his hand! Also, no one had any idea who the "cleaning lady" was who had prayed over Denise.

Because the energy of our healing thoughts has so much effect on others, it is essential that we not only pray for those whom we like and appreciate, but just as importantly, for those whom we need to forgive. When we pray in a non-judgmental way for the enlightenment of others, we are making an immeasurable contribution to the healing of the world. We are also healing our own lives because we are setting up a magnetic field of energy which attracts positive people and situations into our personal lives.

How Can Simply Praying Change the Physical Nature of a Situation?

Although religions have recognized the power of prayer for ages, it is only relatively recently that there is an upsurge of interest on the part of the scientific community to study it. This is most likely because more and more people are reporting experiences of unexplainable, dramatic, even spontaneous healings. The logical, rational aspect of our minds longs to know—how does it work? While there are many studies being documented in an effort to understand how prayer affects physical matter, the power of prayer cannot be locked within the paradigm of scientific justification.

Prayer is on a frequency that resonates with divine light—the same light which is the core essence of each one of us. Because it is an energetic vehicle of unconditional love, prayer has the potential to transform any person and any situation in ways that transcend human rationale. Although I have personally witnessed the miracle of prayer many times within my own life, one instance of spontaneous healing involving my friend, Laura, particularly stands out in my mind.

Laura and I have considered ourselves soul mates (aren't we all!) for most of our lives. A few years ago we went to the seashore together for a few days of rest and relaxation. She said she was feeling extremely stressed because she had just "used every ounce of energy she had" to complete a major project at work. While Laura is a loving and gentle soul who has always been open to listening to my enthusiastic conversations about holistic health, she was generally resistant to believing in natural healing because it ran contrary to her highly driven nature and traditional upbringing. This has never been a problem between us because we have always respected and appreciated how differently we approach life.

Laura was often tired and plagued with physical problems because she tended to ignore her needs for self-nurturing and pushed herself very hard in everything she did. On this day, however, she was especially exhausted and suggested we leave the beach early and return to the room. We loaded ourselves up like pack mules with the usual beach assortment of folding chairs, blankets, bags, and purses and set off to return to our hotel. Laura preceded me in her typical hurried manner as she began to run up the concrete set of stairs to our second-floor room. Suddenly I heard a loud crack and the sound of articles falling all over the place. In horror, I watched Laura smash her head against the concrete wall and fall motionless onto the landing. The sound of her head crashing against the wall was so loud that several people who were inside a room on the lower level heard it and rushed out to see what had happened. They were appalled to learn that what they had heard was the sound of her head colliding into the wall.

Although she was conscious, Laura steadfastly refused to move or be moved for at least twenty minutes. She kept her eyes closed and emphatically repeated the same thing over and over again: "Don't move me and don't call for help. I have to remain still and just listen." There was something strangely calm and convincing in her voice, and so we waited until she agreed to be moved. When she finally stood up she could barely walk, and it took four of us to assist her back to the room. Laura already had a knot on her head the size of a golf ball, a deep bloody gash that ran the entire length of the side of her face, and a knee that was extremely swollen and already bruising.

I walked toward the phone to call a doctor. "No!" she said, "please don't call. Just practice one of your spiritual healing techniques—I am open to whatever you feel guided to do." There was no question about the conviction in her voice. I found myself intuitively responding with a natural healing process called Therapeutic Touch, which works with the body's energy field.

While I usually do Therapeutic Touch with my eyes open, this time I was guided to suggest we both close our eyes and silently pray together while I did it. A few minutes had passed when I heard Laura suddenly say, "Okay—I'm fine now."

I opened my eyes and to my astonishment every trace of injury had disappeared from her body! There was no swelling, no bruises, no bleeding, and no scrapes. In fact, she looked beautiful and totally at peace. "I needed that experience," she said calmly.

"You needed that experience?" I asked in utter amazement.

"Yes, you see the whole time I was lying there I was receiving loving messages. I was told to just remain still and to listen. I was told to pay attention to the message that I had literally and figuratively hit the wall. The message was very consistent: it is time to love myself and to slow down and savor my life. I was reminded that even though I have had a car accident, a serious illness, and two falls this year, I am still not taking care of myself. The message was so loving and gentle . . . to tell you the truth, it was one of the most peaceful experiences I have ever had. I'm not even surprised that all my injuries are healed because while we were praying, I heard these same inner voices tell me that an instantaneous healing was entirely possible—*if I believed* it could happen. I told them . . . '*I believe.*' "

Laura turned her life around that day. Neither one of us can explain it, nor do we even try; but we both know it happened, and we still get tears in our eyes when either of us mentions this awesome and extraordinary experience.

Certainly, not all prayers are answered this dramatically; however, we always receive the responses which are correct for the stage we are at in our soul's evolution when we release our prayers to divine outcomes in the greatest good of all. Sometimes this is difficult for us to understand because healing does not always come in the form of a recovery which coincides with our human success standards. If, for example, it is the will of a person's soul to return to our spiritual home and their work in this life is complete, then the ultimate healing is death. While this may not be the answer we personally hope for, when we are in our correct space of praying in the spirit of neutral, unconditional love we realize that our prayers are answered in accordance with divine will.

When we release our prayers in this way, we had better fasten our seat belts and prepare to witness an extraordinary phenomenon—the universal responses to our prayer requests crop up everywhere we turn. In order to observe how this happens we need to live in a state of *mindfulness*.

What Is Mindfulness?

One of the most exhilarating and fascinating aspects of life is the process of experiencing the generosity of the universe rising to meet our needs and desires. In order to recognize the feedback we are receiving and the forms in which it is appearing, we need to be *mindful*.

When we are mindful, we become keenly observant of everything that is going on in our lives and how it is relevant to our spiritual growth. We transcend our human propensity to unconsciously gulp life by making a conscious choice to savor each delicious moment. Rather than clinging to the past or waiting for the future, we immerse ourselves completely in the unfolding of the present. I imagine mindfulness as spiritual surfing—if we are focusing on where we have been, we lose our balance and fall backwards; if we lean too far forward because we are anxious to get to shore, we fall forwards. And then there is that glorious feeling of just being there, in the perfect space at the perfect time, totally balanced, sensing every nuance of the joy of being effortlessly carried by the waves! Indeed, we are experiencing *mindfulness!*

What Is Synchronicity?

The experience of being in the perfect place at the perfect time, experiencing the joy of universal support in all that we do, is a phenomenon termed by the famed Swiss psychologist, Carl Jung, as *synchronicity*. While at first we may be inclined to dismiss synchronous events as serendipity, happenstance, or luck, the perpetual magical appearance of everything we need whenever we need it is so exciting and so awesome that it defies all earthly explanation!

These responsive messages are delivered into our reality through the synchronous appearances of people, situations, and dreams. Whether it is a parking space opening up exactly when and where we need it, a kind person who shows up out of nowhere to help us in time of danger, a book containing the answer to an important question being placed in our hands by a stranger, a dream offering specific information, or a surprise check in the mail when we weren't sure where our next dollar was coming from, the evidence of universal support is everywhere when our visions and prayers are aligned with divine will. Many times we have only to think a question when the response to it comes out of the mouth of the very next person to whom we speak. It is as though there is a confirming internal presence constantly saying to us, "Yes, you are in your correct space. Keep on doing what you are doing—I support you."

Synchronous messages not only respond to our requests, they also speak to us in the form of kind inner whispers guiding us to take action on things which are in our greatest good. While it is not necessary that we understand the meaning of these intuitive thoughts when we receive them—in fact, we usually don't—it is essential to trust in and act upon them in order to validate their significance. These spiritual messages emerge as spontaneous feelings that we have to do something. Sometimes the messages seem large, such as, we need to quit our jobs; but more often than not, they are seemingly incidental things, such as: making a phone call to a certain person, contributing to a particular social cause, taking an unusual detour while driving somewhere, canceling a meeting, or something as seemingly insignificant as sitting in a particular seat in a restaurant.

What appears to be a small message can have profound significance. A couple of years ago as I was sitting at my desk working, I suddenly felt a strong impulse to go to a little bakery/restaurant in my neighborhood. For at least fifteen minutes, I could think of nothing else. This seemed strange to me because I never had any particular inclination to go to this restaurant before. Also, it was three o'clock in the afternoon—not a time when I would usually have lunch—and I wasn't even hungry.

Nevertheless, I have learned to totally trust these intuitive callings, so I collected myself and headed off to the restaurant. It was a self-serve situation so I put some items on a tray and chose a seat. As I sat down and began to eat, I felt uncomfortable—I was sensing a definite pull to change my table and move toward the window at the front of the restaurant. I decided it best to pick up all my things and move in the direction to which I felt drawn. In the instant I arrived at the window, I was met by the face of a gentleman standing on the outer side of it. It was an old friend whom I had not seen for ten years. I motioned for him to come in.

After we embraced and briefly exchanged amenities, his facial expression quickly became grave. With tears in his eyes he spoke of the excruciating emotional pain he was experiencing and how he had been feeling suicidal for weeks. He said that although he was seeing a doctor and taking medication for his depression, he was sensing the need for a much deeper answer and that, in desperation, he was aimlessly walking around trying to find himself. We spoke for quite a while, even laughing and reminiscing about old times. During the course of our conversation I was able to share with him that I was working in the field of spiritual healing. I offered him my hand and asked him how he felt I could support him.

We got together for weekly healing sessions over the following few months after that meeting, and the ripple of healing that transpired as a result of this "accidental" meeting ushered great inspiration into both our lives. My soul heard his soul crying for help, and I shall always be grateful that I followed my intuition to be in that restaurant on that day, in that specific seat, and at that particular time.

It is our responsibility to be observant of and responsive to these universal clues, for they are truly our guideposts for staying on the path to Oneness. We are here to help each other to learn, to heal, and to grow. The more we pay attention to recognizing the synchronous messages which come to us through the people and situations we encounter in our everyday lives, the more rapidly we are gifted with these magical coincidences. Indeed, this ongoing, persistent revelation of moment-to-moment miracles is splendid verification that when we are being who we truly are, we are completely supported by a kind and supportive universe.

Every day, greater numbers of people are becoming aware of the awesome phenomenon of synchronicity, which is dramatic evidence that our collective consciousness is rapidly awakening and we are moving closer to our spiritual truth. While this is extremely encouraging, we cannot be complacent. Awakening allows no space for going backward. As we remember the truth of our Oneness, it is imperative that we galvanize ourselves into action because we are in the process of a global transformation.

We Are All Part of a Global Transformation

We are on the threshold of the most miraculous change in the experience of humanity. The chaos we are witnessing and experiencing is far more than a periodic transition—a shift from one space to another. **What we are experiencing is a global transformation!** The process of transformation changes not just the *content* but the entire *context* of our existence. Like a caterpillar changing its form before emerging from its cocoon, humanity is changing its entire form as the swell of our spiritual growth is pushing us out of the shell of our outgrown beliefs. Our collective spirit is maturing and internally motivating us to progress beyond a society based solely on the body level of survival and the mental level of ego gratification. We are moving together into the transcendent stage of spiritual unity!

The global disease at the root of all our suffering is *fear*, and the universal vaccine for it is *love*. Every single one of us makes a difference because each loving thought we have is a spark of light that intensifies the illumination of the entire planet. When we pray for the greater good of all humanity, we are living in the spirit of unconditional love, which has the power to transform all that it touches and to dissolve any barriers that divide us. The more we comprehend the true nature of unconditional love, the higher our vibration, and the faster our thoughts manifest as we become clear channels to be healed and to heal others.

Through prayer, we have the collective creative power to transform our present world into a new human reality that reflects the qualities of our true spiritual nature: unconditional love, harmony, wholeness, abundance, and joy. We can all play our part to co-create a World of Oneness by aligning our thoughts with the "A Vision of Oneness" contained on the last page.

I am guided to ask every person who is touched by this book in any way to commit to saying "A Vision of Oneness" at least once every day.

Our thoughts create our reality, so one can only imagine the infinite transformational energy that can be generated by the majority of our world population uniting with each other

I am guided to ask every person who is touched by this book in any way to commit to saying "A Vision of Oneness" at least once every day.

Our thoughts create our reality, so one can only imagine the infinite transformational energy that can be generated by the majority of our world population uniting with each other in a vision prayer for global spiritual healing! While we will find our own unique ways to interpret and express the energy of this "vision of oneness", its intention is to bring a unified spiritual focus to our everyday lives.

Each of us is only responsible to honor our individual role—the rest of how all this happens is up to the infinite potential that lies within the mysteries of the universe transcending the boundaries of time, space, and logic. And the truth is, we don't need to analyze how it will happen because, at a soul level, we already know.

A Vision of Oneness

I *am* at one with The Source of Universal Light
and Ultimate Expression of Universal Love.

I *am* an open, active channel receiving
and expressing unconditional love.

I *am* thankful for all that is.

I am joyfully experiencing peace within,
health at all levels of my being,
and abundance in all forms that are in
my greatest good; and

I see my personal healing contributing to a
World of Unconditional Love, Harmony, Wholeness,
Abundance, and Joy.

I surrender this vision to the unconditional love
of the universe

and know this prayer is answered in ways that are
for the greatest good of all.

Amen.